£12.99

Teaching Children
with Visual Impairments

Open University Press
Children With Special Needs Series

Editors

PHILLIP WILLIAMS
Emeritus Professor of Education
University College of North Wales, Bangor.

PETER YOUNG
Formerly Tutor in the education of children with
learning difficulties; Cambridge Institute of Education;
educational writer, researcher and consultant.

This is a series of short and authoritative introduction for parents, teachers, professionals and anyone concerned with children with special needs. The series will cover the range of physical, sensory, mental, emotional and behavioural difficulties, and the changing needs from infancy to adult life in the family, at school and in society. The authors have been selected for their wide experience and close professional involvement in their particular fields. All have written penetrating and practical books readily accessible to non-specialists.

TITLES IN THE SERIES

Teaching Children with Visual Impairments

Anthony B. Best

Open University Press
Milton Keynes • Philadelphia

Open University Press
Celtic Court
22 Ballmoor
Buckingham
MK18 1XW

and
1900 Frost Road, Suite 101
Bristol, PA 19007, USA

First Published 1992

British Library Cataloguing-in-Publication Data

Best, Anthony B.
  Teaching children with visual impairments.
  –(Children with special needs series)
  I. Title   II. Series
  371.91

  ISBN 0–335–15990–7 (hb)
  ISBN 0–335–15989–3 (pb)

Library of Congress Cataloging-in-Publication Data

Best, Anthony B., 1947—
  Teaching children with visual impairments / Anthony B. Best.
      p.   cm.–(Children with special needs series)
  Includes bibliographical references and index.
  ISBN 0–335–15990–7 (hb).–ISBN 0–335–15989–3 (pb)
  1. Visually handicapped children–Education.   I. Title.
    II. Series
  HV1626.B47   1991
  371.91′ 1–dc20
                                                      91–17912
                                                         CIP

Typeset by Colset Private Limited, Singapore
Printed in Great Britain by St Edmundsbury Press
Bury St Edmunds, Suffolk

Contents

Series Editors' Introduction

We live in a time of great change in education. Public attitudes have altered from an almost unquestioning belief in education as an intrinsic good to a critical doubting of its value, at least as currently practised. This leads to an ancient nostrum: if it doesn't seem to work, reorganize it!

In the UK change has been effected through the 1988 Education Reform Act. This Act standardizes the content of education through the National Curriculum, sets the control of education in the hands of the consumer (the parent, not the child) and structures competition into the system by a funding formula (Local Management of Schools) which will reward high standards of achievement. Two of these three sea-changes sit very uneasily alongside the principles which inform the education of children with special needs, where emphasis has been placed on individual, not uniform educational programmes, and on co-operation, not competition. For these reasons, the recent turmoil in the special-education sector has been even greater than elsewhere. It is argued that the developments now flowing from the introduction of the 1988 Act foreshadow damage to the improvements for which so many special educators worked so devotedly in the years following the 1981 Education Act.

All sectors of special education are having to respond to the changes and challenges of the 1988 Act, including that sector which deals with the education of the visually impaired, the theme of Tony Best's book. But in addition to coping with new legislation, there have been particularly significant changes of a different sort in this sector. The character of the population of children with visual impairment has been altering substantially in recent years. Many children with visual impairment suffer from additional handicaps, and suitable educational programmes have had to be instituted. The nature and format of the educational services available for them have also been altering. Teamwork, using the expertise of members of different professions, has grown. We will have to wait for some time before we can fully appreciate the effects of the profound changes in the structure and management of our educational system on the developments such as these.

One particular development which we hope will survive and strengthen, in spite of the 1988 Act, is the growth in the provision for educating children with visual impairment in ordinary classrooms. For this to be successful, the teacher in the ordinary or 'regular' school must be helped to meet the educational challenges it poses. This book discusses the implications for classroom and school in a most helpful and practical way. Simple yet vitally important issues connected with organizing the educational environment for a child who is visually impaired are explained straightforwardly, often with the help of illustrations. Key topics, such as the development of listening skills, facilitating mobility, the tactile skills needed for reading and writing through Braille, a survey of the advantages and disadvantages of some of the technological aids now available – all these are touched on in later chapters. The text is enlivened with thumbnail sketches of real children presenting real issues which might be met by any teacher or parent in any school. While the book is written at a level which renders it intelligible to non-specialist teachers – a group that includes parents – it is also sufficiently detailed to be a valuable resource for the specialist teacher of the visually impaired

As the book points out, schools for the blind were pioneering ventures in special education, started in many cases before the nineteenth-century acts ensured a broad general education for all. Given this early start, it is not surprising that the education of the visually impaired has developed into a specialized field, with its own skills and its own technologies. This book opens out and explains this field. Everyone in education is likely at some time to meet a child with a visual handicap. This book takes the view that such children are children first and foremost. Their development will be affected by their impairment in different ways, some of which we can readily appreciate, whereas others are less well recognized but need to be understood. These limitations of experience can be alleviated significantly through the use of the insights and approaches that Tony Best's book offers. It will help teachers to help children gain access to a fuller and more satisfying education experience. While we wait to see the full effects of the great changes now affecting the education system, this text will serve as an invaluable handbook of good up-to-date practice in its field.

Phillip Williams
Peter Young

CHAPTER 1

The Basic Concepts

Introduction

A 5-year-old blind girl is in her first day at school. Like some of the other children in the class, she is attending a school for the blind for the first time having previously been at a local nursery. Another newcomer bumps into her as she stands by a table. 'Look out,' she says, 'can't you see I'm blind!' 'Are you?' he says, 'so am I. Why don't you look out?'

A man carrying a white stick is boarding a train. He bumps into the person in front of him several times and some other passengers, noticing his stick, move out of his way. He then takes out his seat reservation, holds it close to his face and looks around for seat numbers. He finds his seat and, turning to the adjacent passenger, says 'Excuse me. I think that is my seat. Could you let me get past you, please?' The other passengers look confused and some are clearly annoyed that a man with a white stick should apparently be able to see.

In talking about people with visual impairments, we are concerned with a heterogeneous group of people who not only have a range of personalities, psychological make-up and interests but also have a wide range of types and degree of visual impairment. The infant described above who is totally blind is one of a small sub-group of the visually impaired. Those with total congenital blindness probably form less than 20 per cent of the total population of children with visual impairments. The man is one of a larger group of those with some useful vision, although within that group are people with very different defects who have different types of residual vision. In his case, perhaps, the type of defect allows him to see quite clearly within a very narrow field of vision but unable to make out large objects such as people. We shall start by examining the medical and legal definitions of blindness and partial sight and then describe some of the differences in residual vision. But before we can examine the idea of subnormal vision, we must first establish what we define as normal vision.

Normal Vision

Those of us who consider we have normal vision are using a standard which is quite arbitrary. We probably mean we can manage perfectly well to do the tasks required of us. A clinical measurement of vision is usually based on the ability to make out letters on an eye chart at a distance of 6 metres. The standard for 'normal' vision is sufficient to allow us to carry out routine activities such as reading telephone directories, driving cars, catching a ball, without visual difficulties. Some people may need better than 'average' vision to carry out their work comfortably. Surgeons and jewellers use vision aids such as magnifiers to help them in some aspects of their work. Many Chinese artists, using extremely fine brushes to make intricate strokes, are myopic or short-sighted and so can see finer detail close to than the 'average' person. Other people may need lower than average levels of vision. Pre-school children, handling brightly coloured toys and large print, may be able to cope perfectly satisfactorily, from a visual point of view, without using their full visual capacity. Many jobs which do not involve reading, from emptying dustbins to reviewing troops, can be carried out without using average visual acuity.

The level of vision is usually expressed as a figure such as 6/6 which indicates the performance of an eye in relation to an average 'good' eye and it is called visual acuity. To obtain a visual acuity, the subject is usually asked to read letters of different sizes from a chart (originally devised in Germany in the 1860s by a Dr Snellen). Each size of letter on the Snellen chart has a number against it and this indicates the distance at which that letter can just be distinguished by an 'average' eye. The test is usually taken at a distance of 6 metres from the chart and the subject asked to name the letters on the chart, starting with the largest. At 6 metres the person with average, or normal, vision should be able to name the letters on one of the lowest lines – the line labelled 6. The largest letter at the top of a chart is numbered 60. If the subject, at 6 metres, can only make out the letters which should be seen at 18 metres they will have a reduced visual acuity which would be expressed as

6 distance of the subject from the test chart
18 smallest size of letter which can be identified.

Average visual acuity is 6/6. (More accurately, the size and shape of the letters are determined by a formula which takes into account both the size of the spaces between components of each letter and the angle that the whole letter makes with the eye.)

Blindness for the lay person usually means total loss of sight. However, the legal definition of blindness, used by the Department of Social Security (DSS) for the purpose of obtaining benefits, means something different. It is based on a person's ability to see the letters on the Snellen acuity chart. Blindness is defined as an acuity of less than 3/60 in the better eye with correction. This score represents a performance by the child of being able to make out the largest letter on the chart at 3 metres, or less than that. Certainly not total blindness, and there may be considerable useful vision for close work and for mobility with an acuity of even 1/60. About 80 per cent of children classed as legally blind on this criterion have some useful vision. While this remaining vision may sometimes not be very helpful to an elderly person, it is enormously significant for children who may benefit from training in interpreting the very imperfect or incomplete images they see. Over the past fifteen years, training residual vision has become an important part of many educational programmes for children with visual impairments. There is, therefore, an important difference between the medical and educational concepts of blindness.

From an educational point of view, blindness means total absence of sight. It presents a set of needs and difficulties which, to some extent, are different from those experienced by other people with visual impairments: for example, using touch to explore objects, reading and writing in braille, having voice only for identifying speakers, being dependent on information from a white cane for mobility. But in practice the situation is very much more complex, for some people with partial sight will also function as blind people in some situations where their level of vision is inadequate, perhaps in poor lighting. Many other people will use touch and vision together in their daily lives, for example, to confirm that there is nothing on a chair seat or to establish their blouse or collar is properly adjusted.

Total Blindness

Total blindness is either congenital or acquired. The difference is important for, if the onset of blindness has occurred after 5 years of age, then the child will almost certainly have some visual memories which may help in imagining and understanding many concepts. In particular, it may be helpful in enabling the child construct an image of the space around him and this should lead to easier orientation and mobility than for the congenitally blind child. If children lose their sight before this age, there is ample anecdotal evidence that some useful visual memory might remain. This is unlikely to be the case if vision is lost before the age of 18 months.

Partial Sight

The majority of children who are visually impaired have some remaining or residual vision. Like blindness, the term 'partial sight' has a precise legal definition which is a visual acuity of between 3/60 and 6/60. For *educational* purposes the term has always been interpreted to mean children with a significant visual handicap and, while this has very roughly corresponded to an acuity of less than 6/60, it has included children with acuities above and below the legal range. Why is there this discrepancy between educational and legal definitions? The reasons are crucial to the understanding of visual handicap and the educational implications of the impairment.

Firstly, the acuity score is determined by performance on the task of identifying a stationary black-on-white image at a distance. Children in school need many other visual skills, and performance on the acuity test will not necessarily equate with performance at these other tasks. Children need to see near objects, moving objects, objects in different lighting conditions. They need to be able to see while moving about and to change focus from one object to another. While these tasks may not cause difficulty for those with near normal vision, children with severely reduced acuity and, possibly, additional handicap may well have particular problems in some of these areas.

Secondly, the effects of different visual defects can be quite specific and cover a wide range of practical difficulties. Some defects result in clear vision only in darker than average lighting, others in lighting levels which are unusually high; some result in clear near vision but total blindness for distant tasks; some allow for sharp distance vision but over a very narrow visual field and almost no useful vision for reading. The acuity score does not take this range of difficulties into account.

Thirdly, the use an individual can make of his remaining vision seems to vary according to experience, expectations and psychological make-up. While this use of vision can often be improved by training, we still have no full understanding of these perceptual and individual factors in seeing.

The author knows of two adults with identical acuity scores of 1/60. One cycles, not very safely, to work and teaches physical education to handicapped children. The other uses a white cane to help him travel. Both read braille. They have different eye diseases and have had their impairment for different lengths of time. One calls himself partially sighted, the other says he is blind. Both are part of the population of people with visual impairments. This example illustrates the way these factors interact to confound the simpler concepts of blindness and partial sight.

Function of the Eye and Eye Defects

In order to gain a better understanding of the nature of residual vision we need to examine the causes of visual defects. How does the eye work and what can go wrong with it? In some ways this is only part of the question we should ask for it is the process of seeing, which involves the eyeball and the rest of the brain, which we need to examine in order to pinpoint the effect of an eye defect on a child. The process of seeing involves receiving light signals in the eye, transmitting that information to the visual cortex and interpreting that information once it has been processed by the cortex. If something goes wrong with any part of that process, the child will have difficulty seeing. Therefore we need to understand a little about all parts of the process and this will be particularly important with multi-handicapped children as they may have specific difficulty

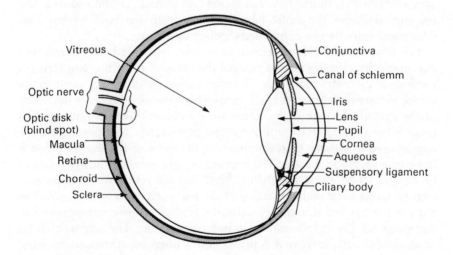

Figure 1.1 Horizontal section of a right eyeball.

interpreting the partial and inconsistent information they receive through
their eyes.

Clear but detailed descriptions of the eye and common defects are
included in a number of recent publications including Jan, Freeman and
Scott (1977); Dobree and Boulter (1982); Jose (1983); Fitt and Mason
(1986). Any of those descriptions will complement the outline given
here.

The process of seeing starts at the outer surface of the eyeball, the
cornea. This curved surface is responsible for about 80 per cent of the
focusing needed to enable us to see clearly (the lens deals with the 'fine'
focusing). Scarring on the cornea, usually caused by accidents, can inter-
fere with the passage of light rays and results in blurred vision or distorted
images. Astigmatism is caused by irregularities on the surface of the
cornea, again resulting in slightly distorted or blurred images. Astigmatism can usually be corrected by glasses but, if uncorrected, may cause
difficulties in judging distances – reaching for objects, judging depth –
and in seeing small objects clearly at any distance.

Behind the cornea is a space filled with clear liquid, the aqueous. This
liquid is drained out of eye by the Canal of Schlemm which is a circular
vein around the edge of the cornea. As fresh liquid is generated in the
eyeball, so the older liquid drains out of the eye to maintain an acceptable
pressure within the eyeball. If a build-up of liquid occurs, either through a
blockage of the canal or through over-production of liquid, the pressure
in the eye increases and damage can occur. This is glaucoma. When it is
congenital, it is called 'Buphthalmos'. The elevated pressure can cause
severe headaches, blurred overall vision and ultimately blind spots as the
pressure damages the optic nerve leading from the back of the eye.
Glaucoma can often be controlled through eyedrops.

The *iris*, usually coloured blue or brown, is behind the cornea and
automatically changes size to control the amount of light going through
the hole at its centre. The hole, the *pupil*, appears as a black circle in the
centre of the eye. It appears black simply because we usually see the inside
of the eyeball through it and there is no light in there. In photographs
taken with a flash gun or with a narrow beam torch, that part of the eye
appears red as we are then illuminating the back of the eye and that is
covered with blood vessels. The amount of light entering the eye needs to
be controlled to allow the delicate cells on the retina to function efficiently. Congenital malformations of the iris, such as coloboma, result in
gaps in the iris and this causes defective central vision corresponding to
the shape of the coloboma. It is not correctable. The apparent total
absence of the iris is termed Aniridia and is often accompanied by other
congenital abnormalities. A lack of pigment in the iris, which can be seen
as a very pale blue or pinky iris, is one form of albinism. The sufferer is

usually very sensitive to light and needs to wear dark glasses. Lack of adequate control of the light entering the eye results in difficulties in focusing and nystagmus, an involuntary movement of the eyeball.

Directly behind the iris is the *lens*. It is held in position by the ciliary muscles and these contract and expand to change the shape of the lens. The lens is responsible for focusing images on to the retina and the automatic action of the muscles enables us to see clearly from just a few inches up to infinity. One of the most common causes of visual impairment is cataract. This occurs when, for some reason, a portion of the lens becomes opaque and prevents the passage of light on to the retina. This results in an interrupted field of vision which, if there is a central opacity, will severely impair vision. The cause of many congenital cataracts is not understood, although they can occur if the foetus has been infected, for example with rubella, during the first three months of pregnancy, when the eye is forming. Cataracts can also be hereditary. Treatment may be through a needling operation in which a needle is inserted into the lens allowing acqueous to enter the lens and break the fibres causing the opacity. More commonly, the lens is removed. The resulting eye is known as aphakic and glasses will be needed to help in focusing. Usually two pairs are prescribed, one for near and one for distant viewing.

The lens may be dislocated or partly dislocated (subluxated). In this condition the muscles holding the lens become detached, usually through a congenital weakness but occasionally through an accident. The lens is displaced or falls behind the iris into the body of the eyeball. The result is a loss of clear vision and often complications such as glaucoma.

The back of the eyeball is covered, right up to the cornea, with the *retina*, an incredible layer of 126 million separate cells, each linked, through fibres in the optic nerve, to the visual cortex of the brain. These cells are sensitive to light and undergo a chemical change when light falls on them. This change is converted into electrical energy and transmitted through the optic nerve to a section of the cortex which deals with information from a specific part of the retina. The cells are of two main types. Cones are grouped mainly at the centre of our field of vision and are used to see detail. Rods, which form the majority of cells, are particularly responsible for vision in low levels of lighting. There are about 6 million cones in the eye although the 2,000 at the centre of our field, the macula, are the ones used to see fine detail. Almost each one of these cones is connected by its own fibre to a section of the visual cortex where information from that cone is analysed. A large amount of space in the visual cortex is given over to the information coming from these cones and this results in the brain being able to see clearly the detail of objects 'viewed' by the macula. Damage to just a few of these 2,000 cones can greatly impair our vision. Vision peripheral to those central few degrees is much less clear. We may be aware of shapes and colours but cannot, for example, read with our more peripheral vision. This part of the retina is made up of around 120 million rods, with cones interspersed amongst them. Rods cannot 'see' colours and are very sensitive to light. This makes them particularly useful for seeing at night, although in ordinary lighting they function less well than cones. Why do we see less well in these peripheral areas? The reason is not to do with the characteristics of rods and cones so much as what happens behind them. The optic nerve consists of about one million fibres each connected to rods and cones. But whereas many fibres serving the macula area are attached to only one cell, fibres in the peripheral area are connected to hundreds and sometimes thousands of cells. Thus the information from those areas is much less precise and our vision is much less clear. In general, the number of cells connected to a fibre increases the further the area is from the macula.

The retinal cells are complex and a number of congenital and hereditary problems can affect them. One group of disorders are the tapetoretinal degenerations. Retinitis pigmentosa is the term used for a family of these hereditary degenerative conditions. They result, initially, in loss of function of the peripheral rods causing a narrowed field of vision and particular difficulty seeing in dark conditions. As the disease progresses, the field of vision narrows ('tunnel vision') and, usually during the teenage years or early twenties, results in very severe loss of vision. There is no known treatment. Retinitis pigmentosa (RP) can also occur with congenital deafness in a condition known as Usher's Syndrome. Other disorders in this group include Leber's Amaurosis and Batten's Syndrome.

Macula degeneration is, in some ways, the opposite of RP as central vision is first affected. This immediately causes a significant handicap to the sufferer, removing the clear central vision and leaving only blurred peripheral vision which cannot be aided by glasses. Diabetes in children can result in damage throughout the retina and may result in total blindness. An added complication of this condition is the associated loss of feeling in the fingers which can make the use of braille very difficult. A detached retina occurs when a piece of the retina tears and becomes detached from the layers behind it. This results in loss of vision over the area of the tear, although, with a small tear, this may not cause a major handicap. Treatment is through the use of lasers to reattach the flap of retina. This condition is often associated with high myopia in which the elongated shape of the eyeball causes the retina to be stretched very thinly around the back of the eyeball.

The *optic nerve* runs from the eyeball through the skull to the visual cortex (although for the second part of this route it is called a tract). The nerves from each eye meet about two inches behind the eyeball and there is cross-over of some of the fibres so that those connected to the same half of each retina travel together into the visual cortex. The brain can then compare the slightly different information on the position of an object which comes from each eye and thus make a decision about the precise position of objects. This enables us to have stereoscopic vision. The term 'optic atrophy' is used to describe a partial or complete loss of function of the optic nerve and is the most common defect causing blindness in children. It results in loss of vision, the nature of which is determined by the fibres which are no longer transmitting information. Optic atrophy can occur as a congenital condition for which, usually, no cause can be identified. It can occur as a condition secondary to a tumour or glaucoma in which pressure on the optic nerve cuts off the blood supply and results in permanent damage. It can be caused by an infection such as meningitis or an inflammation such as multiple sclerosis. Once the fibres have been damaged, it is not possible to regenerate them. A major cause of blindness in the 1950–60s, and one which re-emerged to a lesser extent in the mid-1980s, is retrolental fibroplasia. The condition is now termed retino-pathy of prematurity (ROP). This is damage to the fibres of the optic nerve resulting, in part, from the use of pure oxygen in premature babies. The oxygen arrests the development of the fibres and, when the infant is removed into normal atmosphere, the over-rapid burst of growth results in a malformed nerve. The amount of oxygen given to an infant is critical. Birth weight is a rough guide to a safe dosage, but individuals vary in their susceptibility in an unpredictable way. In addition, there are clearly other unidentified factors involved and, until these have been established, ROP seems likely to remain a cause of impairment in premature children. ROP often cause total blindness in both eyes, although partial damage to the optic nerves will result in uncorrectable blurred vision with some inter-ruption in the visual field.

Our knowledge of the visual cortex increased dramatically during the 1970s and early 1980s, largely through the work of David Marr in Massachusetts and two neurophysiologists, Hubel and Weisel, who were awarded a Nobel prize for their discoveries. It is now known that the cortex is made up of cells arranged in columns, and clusters of these columns, called hypercolumns, sort out the information coming from one area, a hyperfield, of the retina. Individual cells within a hypercolumn give off an electrical charge if a very specific type of activity takes place within the related field of the retina. Although we do not yet have a complete understanding of the function of the cells, it seems that some respond only to a dark/light horizontal edge within the field. Other cells respond to vertical or diagonal lines; others to movement in a specific direction; others to angles within the field. What is clear is that this complicated reorganization of the information coming from the retina results ultimately in our being able to 'see' an object – to recognize it and associate with it a multitude of emotions, qualities and characteristics. What is not clear is how and where this recognition takes place. The visual cortex, which was once assumed to be the interpretive centre, now seems to be just a staging post in the transmission of information to an interpretive centre.

Mentally handicapped children may have a problem interpreting the information coming out of the visual cortex and, when this information is incomplete because of a visual impairment, the child may not be able to deduce what they are seeing. This may discourage attempts to use vision. It may also make visual performance erratic from day to day as factors such as tiredness, drugs, unclear visual environment and inappropriate lighting cause too great a visual problem to be solved. The threshold for confusion in visual interpretation will be low compared to that of a non-handicapped child.

There are two eye conditions involving the whole eyeball which commonly cause significant visual impairments. The eyeball should be roughly a spherical shape but it is sometimes elongated or flattened. This means the distance between the lens and retina is abnormally long or short and, in either case, the lens is not powerful enough to focus light rays on the retina. The result is blurred vision for objects at some distances. If the eyeball is elongated the condition is termed myopia. Near objects can be seen clearly but those further away will be out of focus. Glasses can help in many cases; indeed the majority of spectacle wearers have some degree of myopia. But high myopia is too severe for complete correction and is a common cause of partial sight. The condition is congenital, and sometimes hereditary, but is often not recognized until the child is several years old and is having difficulty at play and in school work. The opposite condition, hypermetropia, results in difficulty in seeing near objects.

Nystagmus is an involuntary rapid movement of the eyeballs. It is often secondary to conditions causing difficulties in fixating and forming a clear retinal image, such as congenital cataracts, albinism or optic atrophy. Nystagmus can also be a condition in itself resulting from a congenital abnormality in controlling muscle movement. It causes poor vision, although the brain usually suppresses the vision during eye movement and uses only the stationary phase for seeing.

This overview of the way the eye works should also have given an indication of the range of difficulties that can be caused by visual impairment. Partial sight is clearly not simply an overall blurring of vision. There may be central or peripheral problems; there may be an interrupted field or a narrow field; there may be difficulties with close work or with distant viewing; glasses may help in some cases but not in others; some conditions result in better acuity in dark conditions and sensitivity to light, while others need high levels of lighting for good vision.

In discussing the physical causes of vision difficulties, we have covered only part of the process. Once information has been sorted out in the visual cortex, it is then sent further into the brain to be interpreted. This psychological part of the process has been examined in some detail although there are many aspects which are still not understood. What happens, though, is very evident for we are each able to recognize much of what our eyes look at and, within a fraction of a second, name, remember, associate, feel and react to the image. This perceptual part of the process may be more difficult if the information being received in the interpretative centre is incomplete, inconsistent or ambiguous. The brain may be unable to conclude what is being looked at, may take a longer time than normal to reach a decision or come to the wrong decision. If it is known that a familiar object or action is being looked at, then the number of possibilities are fewer and so a decision can be made with less information. This might be the case, for example, if the object viewed must be one of two or three familiar people, if the viewer is in a familiar playground where there are known swings, roundabout and climbing frames. The decision may also be easier if other sensory information, for example sounds, are present to aid in the interpretation of the visual information.

Assessment of Vision

There are likely to be several aspects of vision which are examined in a clinical assessment. These are the ability to see clearly, both near and at a distance, the field of vision and the appearance of the eye. A variety of procedures can be used to collect information on these aspects and some common procedures are described below.

Before any detailed examination is needed, a child will go through a screening test to identify the possibility of a visual difficulty. This may take place at a children's clinic, playgroup, nursery, school or at general practitioner's surgery. It is often carried out by orthoptists who are specially trained to deal with the screening and assessment of vision. For children able to match or read, a Snellen eyechart or variation of it can be used. This gives a preliminary acuity score. The variations include charts with outlines of common objects, rather than letters, which the child has to name or match to similar shapes on a card he is given. A simplified letter chart is one of the procedures included in the Stycar vision tests – a set of procedures for acuity and screening assessment which can be used by medical staff, psychologists and qualified teachers of the visually impaired.

The miniature-toys test is part of the Stycar procedures, designed to screen children who are not ready to use letter charts. A set of toys – miniature doll, chair, knife, fork and spoon – are individually held up at 3 metres from the child and he is asked to name the object or indicate what it is by pointing to a similar set in front of him. Failure to distinguish the difference between the smallest items – the spoon and the fork – would suggest the need for further examination. Younger children, from about 6 months, can be screened with the rolling-ball test. The child is seated on the floor and then a small white ball is rolled along his field of vision at a distance of about 3 metres. The child is expected to fixate on the ball when it becomes stationary. If he is not able to do this, a visual problem might be suspected. These screening procedures need great care in administration and in the interpretation of the results if they are to provide reliable information. If a child is referred for further examination, he may have a detailed test of visual acuity and field-of-vision assessment. The vision of each eye would be examined as well as both eyes together. This examination may possibly use some other parts of the Stycar procedures.

Included in the set is a commonly used procedure which requires the child to look at white balls of differing sizes held in front of a black background. At 3 metres the balls, mounted on black sticks, are moved individually in front of the screen and the tester observes the child's reaction through a hole in the screen. Although the size of the balls very roughly equate to acuity scores, the test requires the ability simply to observe the presence of the balls rather than to discriminate between and identify shapes as in the letter charts. It therefore presents a rather different type of task to the child.

Another part of the Stycar procedures consists of cards with single letters on them and this mode of presentation may be easier for some children than viewing a complete chart. The cards can also be used at 3 metres rather than the more usual 6 metres and this can help in building up a rapport with pre-school children. For children with very low levels of vision, the Panda test is an extension of the single-letter cards. It consists of a set of white shapes on a black background, some slightly larger than the '60' letter on a Snellen chart. There is also a set of plastic shapes which can be felt. These materials can be used at any distance to collect information about the extent of a child's vision, particularly in cases where standard testing has been unable to record an acuity.

Near vision must also be measured and this can be done using a version of the letter charts on which there are smaller shapes or, for those children able to read, a set of simple stories in different size print (the Maclure Reading Test). A recent test published by a Swedish ophthalmologist, Eva Lindstedt, is designed to help in the assessment of near vision of visually impaired children. Acuity scores have been obtained from this as low as 0.5/60. However, this material can also be used to obtain more detailed information on a child's performance. The material consists of a set of cards (about playing card size) on which are printed black shapes of objects. The size of the pictures varies. The objects have been selected so that some are very similar visually (e.g. pair of scissors, glasses; clock-face/wheel). The cards can be given to a child for sorting or matching and the visual and perceptual-cognitive elements of the task can be varied by careful selection of the cards. Visually, it is useful to establish the child's threshold of performance for similar-looking pictures. However, it may also be useful to find out if he is able to differentiate between smaller pictures if the objects are quite dissimilar (e.g. fork, clock-face). If the child has very low levels of vision, it may be possible for him to distinguish between only the largest dissimilar pictures. Collecting this type of information is part of the work of the teacher of the visually impaired and can lead to suggestions for appropriate classroom materials and teaching approaches for a child.

Very young children, under a year old, may be assessed using their preferential looking behaviour. Young children seem to have a preference for looking at clear-cut patterns rather than a blank screen (Atkinson and Braddick 1979). Therefore a card, with black and white stripes on it, is presented to the child at the same time as a blank card. An observation is made of the child's eye movements and, if the child persistently prefers the striped card, it is assumed he can see the pattern. A series of cards with stripes of different thicknesses and contrast can be presented to find the threshold at which the infant no longer seems to prefer one target card to the other. This indicates that he can no longer see any difference in the cards. Although an acuity score can be obtained from this procedure, it may be more useful to give information about general visual functions (Hyvarinen 1988). A similar approach has been used by teachers with mentally handicapped children to provide an informal assessment and to stimulate vision. Some success for this method has been noted (Bell 1983).

Another part of the assessment at this stage is likely to be field of vision. Full vision allows us to see horizontally over roughly 170°, almost in line with each shoulder but with some defects the field of vision is narrowed. A crude estimation of the field can be made using Stycar balls mounted on sticks and moved up and down to the side of the child. The position at which the child first notices the balls, while he is looking straight ahead, should be the same on each side and be slightly in front of the shoulder. An asymmetrical pattern would indicate visual difficulty in one eye. A more accurate assessment can be made, by qualified medical personnel using a perimeter. The patient is asked to indicate when he first sees a small point of light which is brought forward from behind him over the whole visual field of 360°. The visual field can then be plotted for each eye and any deficiencies identified.

Two other aspects of vision may be assessed at this stage, although neither is likely to be the central concern of the teacher of the visually impaired. Colour-vision defects, unusual in girls but occurring in around 8 per cent of boys, can be identified using the Isahara or City University tests. Tests for muscle imbalance causing squints, an area covered very thoroughly by orthoptists, can be carried out by assessing the position of each eye and the child's ability to use binocular vision.

Finally, the concept of contrast sensitivity emerged during the 1980s as potentially an important aspect of vision and one that seemed at least part-ially independent of acuity. To see objects, the eye has to be aware of edges through discerning the contrast between adjacent surfaces or between foreground and background. A person's ability to detect these differences can be measured and experimental results indicate that this aspect of seeing is significant in understanding the nature of residual vision and in predict-ing what viewing conditions and materials are most appropriate for an individual (Hyvarinen 1983). The tests involve looking at gratings with differing degrees of contrast and establishing the threshold at which the contrast between lines is so low that it cannot be seen.

A third aspect of assessment is the clinical examination by an ophthalmologist, a doctor specializing in eye defects and eye surgery. His examination may involve some of the acuity measurements already described but will concentrate on an examination of the eye to look for indications of disease or malformation. The cornea, iris, lens and retina will all be examined and he may order supplementary electrical tests to provide more information about the retina, optic nerve and visual cortex. The electrical tests record the response of the retina (electroretinogram) or the visual cortex (visually evoked response) to a flash of light. Electrodes on the scalp measure electrical activity and this can indicate the condition of each part of the retina or the extent to which the optic nerve is trans-mitting information to the visual cortex. Early changes in these organs can be detected before they have any significant effect on vision.

Role of Vision

How does lack of vision affect the child's development? What are the educational implications of blindness and partial sight? We can start to examine this by thinking about the role of vision in learning.

Total or partial lack of vision inevitably creates difficulties in under-standing the world. Vision, one of our two distance senses, is a major source of information for us from a very early age. It is a coordinating sense. It enables us to be aware of near and distant objects and the relationships between them in position. We can see most of the furniture in a room at one glance and understand where each piece is located; we can work out the route we are going to take across a shopping precinct by seeing the shop we are aiming for and all the obstacles in the way; young children can see other human beings and notice how their bodies are put together and the movements each part can make. Consider this example of use of vision by a baby.

Imagine a 5-month-old baby at play. He is sitting up on a carpet surrounded by toys. A radio is playing in the background. He looks towards a yellow sponge ball and tries to grasp it. He watches it roll away and then turns his attention to a yellow plastic duck near his other hand. He glances back at the yellow ball, as if comparing the two objects. He successfully picks up the duck and bangs it on the carpet. By accident, he bangs it against some wooden bricks. It makes a quite different sound and he stops for a moment and then continues to bang it against the bricks. A new tune starts on the radio and he looks round to find the source of the music. His mother comes into the room and he glances at her as she smiles at him. 'Do you like that tune?' she asks and he watches as she bends over the radio and moves the sliding control which alters the volume. He glances back at her face and smiles, then lifts up his arms as she walks towards him to pick him up.

Let us examine this sequence again, concentrating on the role of vision. Bear in mind how different the experience might be for a child with a visual impairment. As the child sits on the floor his vision, a coordinating sense, enables him to see the walls, ceiling and furniture and the relationship between them. He is aware of objects he cannot touch, such as the ceiling light, and can judge which objects are near and which are further away. He can work out which objects are in front of others, perhaps a settee in front of a wall or a chair partly hiding the floor which is behind it. As he looks around at his toys – the bricks, a duck, a ball – he can decide which one he would prefer to play with and use his developing hand–eye coordination to reach the correct distance in the right direction to grasp the ball. His decision to reach for the ball might be because it was nearest, or the most attractive colour, or that it seemed the most potential fun. As he fails to grasp it and it rolls away, he can see why he can no longer touch it and perhaps work out an alternative strategy, involving the use of both hands, which might overcome the difficulty he had in gripping it with his little fingers. His vision will have enabled him to have the experience of seeing the ball roll and, later, he may be able to compare that movement with what happens after he drops one of the bricks. With the ball now out of reach, he looks for something else to occupy him and in a quick glance can see several alternatives. Perhaps it is the bright colour, the shining surface, the overall shape, or even the smile painted on the face which attracts him to the duck. He reaches directly for the beak, judges it the right size for his grasp and, holding it firmly, lifts it up. He will see, but will not be aware, that the whole shape changes as he lifts it and turns it. Unlike a child who explores through touch, he will already accept that a toy can appear different but actually remain the same object. He watches his hand, arm and duck all move up and down as he bangs the duck against the carpet and can anticipate the moment the sound is made as the duck and carpet come together. The unexpected sound of duck against brick may surprise him momentarily but he can use his vision instantly to check what has happened. He then confirms his suspicions by repeating the movement against the brick. When his mother enters the room, he can see her whole body moving – walking, bending, reaching out. This will help him build up an understanding of his own body and how it can move.

At 5 months, his main interest is likely to be the area around him but his vision enables him to keep in contact with what is happening further away. A few months later, his interest will have extended to the whole room and his vision will be crucial in encouraging him to crawl as he spots objects he wants to play with or explore.

Even at this early age then, vision is vital to the child in his development. He is using his vision to direct his reaching and monitor his finger movements as he tries to grasp objects. He can monitor the effect of his behaviour on other people by looking at their faces. He is able to notice the link between cause and effect as he sees a ball he touches roll away, an object he hits make a noise, a control on the radio altered and the sound become louder. He is stimulated into activity and movement by looking around and spotting toys he would like to play with or actions he would like to copy. He can compare objects and note their similar colours, differences in shape; he can see how they change their appearance as they are turned around or, with people, how they can bend, stretch or move around. He can anticipate what is going to happen by watching two objects come closer together or by seeing someone about to pick him up.

Even in a few minutes' activity we can see the way in which vision has a central role in enabling a child to monitor, compare, anticipate, understand cause and effect and gain stimulation. These are all vital to his development. It will come as no surprise that children with visual impairment often show a developmental lag in many areas. That lag can be clearly measured as early as 6 months and it may be quite pronounced by 12 months. The lag is not inevitable and appropriate early intervention can overcome many of the difficulties in some areas of development, but without clear vision the process of development is likely to be delayed. Most studies in the past few years, though, have concluded that the *pattern* of development may well be the same for children with and without visual impairments. The area of motor development may be an exception to this rule, but there is insufficient evidence from research studies to be certain of what to expect. Even the authoritative digest of research on early development by Warren (1984), which runs to some 300 pages, has to conclude that there is a serious need for more information.

Effects of Visual Impairment

Visual impairment is likely to affect all areas of development. If we examine, briefly, a few specific areas, we can appreciate the types of difficulty which might arise. Motor development is of particular concern and this includes the element of movement and of orientation. The child cannot easily *monitor* his movement and so may have difficulty understanding what happens when he moves or stretches a limb, bends at the waist or rolls over. If he is not able to see other people clearly, he will have no model to *copy*. He may not realize what 'sitting up straight' is, how to 'march like a soldier', what are acceptable body movements and how mannerisms such as rocking or head rolling may appear. Without clear vision there may be *orientation* problems caused by a difficulty in creating a mental map of his surroundings. For example, he may not know which direction to go to find the door, toy, biscuit or parent. He may not know how to find his way round obstacles to get to his goal. Uncertainties about his surroundings may lead to a lack of *confidence* in moving. The experience of unsuccessful or painful attempts to find his way around may further exacerbate this difficulty. And finally, lack of effective vision may remove an important source of *motivation* for a child. There may not be attractive objects to encourage him to attempt to crawl across a room or to reach out to a mobile over his head. Reaching to sound, which is possible for children with visual impairment, is more complex than visually directed reaching and usually occurs at a later stage of development. So visually handicapped children typically show delays in motor development. This has been quantified by Reynell (1978) who established a delay beginning at about 6–8 months and continuing throughout the pre-school years. At the age of 5, the children in their sample were, on average, 12 months behind sighted children.

Language development may also be affected. The sequence of development may be the same as for sighted children, although the route the blind child uses to move between stages, and the age at which developments take place, may be affected. In particular, the meaning that children with visual impairments attach to words needs to be considered.

A 4-year-old blind girl was playing in the hallway of her house and moved to the kitchen door. She called out to her mother who was working in the kitchen, 'Can you see me?' Her mother turned around and said she could. Then the girl moved to the bottom of the stairs and again asked the question of her mother. She turned round and called out 'Yes, dear, I can still see you.' Then the child went under the stairs and crouched in the corner of the space between the stairs and the floor. Again she called out 'Can you see me now?' Her mother turned round and, not being able to see her daughter, said 'No, of course not, where have you gone?' 'Oh, I can see *you!*' the little girl replied. The girl, it could be interpreted, was experimenting with the meaning of the word 'see'. She has an understanding of it which seemed to equate with being in 'contact with' but was beginning to realize that for other people the meaning must be different. It would be some time before she could understand the concept of vision being dependent on a straight line without obstruction.

Although children with visual impairment will use many other words appropriately, they may attach a slightly different meaning based perhaps on their tactile and auditory experiences (consider the words 'car', 'horse', 'fire'). Other words will be used without direct experience of the concept they represent, such as 'ceiling', 'moon', 'horizon', 'gallop'. Even those words which they can fully understand, such as 'chair', 'knife', 'cup', 'shirt' will be based on contact with a more limited range of examples than for sighted children. Imagine the number of cups that a sighted 4-year-old has experienced. Not only those he has touched and used, but hundreds more he has seen in his house, friends' houses, shops, books, on television. His concept of 'cups' is likely to be wider than a blind child's and include a greater variety of shapes, sizes, colours and materials. In these respects, language development will be affected by the presence of visual impairment. Other aspects of language such as the use of questions, personal pronouns and articulation will be examined later.

Social skills and emotional development can also be affected by visual impairment. Older children may need some help in using body language, establishing social distance in conversation, developing an appropriate dress sense. Consider this example of the sort of doubts and uncertainties a blind 7-year-old boy was living with. It is recorded in an article by psychologist Doris Wills (1981: 219).

> When I was driving 7-year-old Sam home on a bumpy road, he asked me, 'Was that a baby you ran over just now?' When Sam was under 3 he was in a major car accident in which relatives were killed. While this would have traumatised a sighted child, he would have been reassured by observing hundreds of vehicles driven safely as he grew older. This enables the sighted child to put the early experience in some kind of proportion. Insofar as aggression motivates such a question, the sighted child would

express it in a much more displaced way. He could not misunderstand the happenings to this frightening degree. Such a mistaken assumption, in Sam's case about the behaviour of his objects, lays the ground for further misunderstanding.

Wills also records the difficulty in object constancy that some blind infants experience without vision. They may have difficulty understanding that their mother is a person who can scold them and be the same person who loves them. They need extra clues to reassure them that the person is constant and is simply displaying different aspects of her personality.

Learning without Vision

Our earlier example of an infant playing with toys gives us information about another aspect of visual impairment – its effect on the nature of learning. Imagine a blind infant exploring a sponge block, plastic duck or even mother. Both the sighted and blind infant may be able to identify each object and recognize some common features in their explorations. But the nature and quality of the explorations are likely to be different. The blind child, lacking the coordinating sense of vision, will need to examine elements of even quite small objects in a sequential manner. He will move his fingers from one part of the object to another, returning to check the relationship of parts and then trying to imagine how they must fit together. For larger objects, like a person or a chair, this can be a complex task and one that takes a lot more time than a quick visual exploration. The child with poor vision may also have to explore elements of an object sequentially as his vision will not allow him to see the detail of a whole object in one glance.

As the blind child runs his finger over the object, say the yellow plastic duck, the qualities which strike him may be different from those that would occur to the sighted child. Perhaps it would be the smoothness and hardness rather than the bright yellow colour that is of interest to him. A squeaky bear might appeal to a sighted child because of the cheerful smile and big eyes, while the blind child might enjoy it primarily because of the sound it makes. The sighted infant may get a lot of pleasure from a colourful mobile over his cot but the feel of the separate pieces may have very little attraction to a blind child. As well as different qualities of objects being of interest, different elements may carry useful information. The blind child may recognize a tube of toothpaste, not by its overall shape and the coloured wording on the side, but by the feel of the top, the crimped base of the tube and the smell. Both sighted and blind children can successfully identify the tube and its contents but use different features to do so. The partially sighted child may need to use both touch and vision to be sure of correctly identifying some objects.

Although both children will be able to identify many objects and activities, in almost every situation the quantity and quality of the information will be reduced for the child with visual impairment and he will have to work harder to interpret his surroundings. There will be occasions when the information available will not be sufficient to enable the child to understand what is happening. Both aspects of this factor – the quantity and quality of information – need to be considered if we are to understand how best to help a child with visual impairments. The *quantity* of information available is often less for a sighted child. Judgements about a person, for example, may have to be based on his voice and conversation rather than on these qualities in addition to eyes, smile, physique, clothes and body language. A screech of brakes followed by a crash may be enough to deduce that an accident has taken place but not sufficient to know what the result was and if people were injured. For the fully sighted person the amount of information available generally means that some of it is redundant. A door opens, footsteps are heard and the visitor says hello. Sighted people look up to confirm who has entered the room. If they had not heard the greeting, they could still have checked using vision. No such option is available to many people with visual impairments. There is less redundancy in the information they have access to and, if they had missed the greeting, would have had to engineer a situation to identify the person. For children in a busy classroom, instructions, incidents, accidents and opportunities can come piling one on top of another. Interpreting all that with limited vision can be hard work.

Not only is less information available but less useful information may be available – the *quality* of the information is reduced. Compare the information available from listening to water being poured into a glass with seeing the mass of water change shape, the flow alter with the angle of the jug, the sparkle and froth of the water. The blind infant with the yellow duck can bang it on the floor and feel its smoothness but imagine the quality of his playing compared with that of the child who can see the duck change shape as he holds it, can anticipate the noise it might make as he moves it towards different objects and can check his toy against pictures of the real thing.

One important consequence of this reduction in the quantity and quality of information can be difficulty in copying others and in learning incidentally. Much of our learning, as children and as adults, is incidental. Even in the classroom, children have valuable lessons from each other not only in how to behave but also in solving problems set by the teacher. In the pre-school years, important experiences are assimilated which are used to acquire concepts such as conservation. A newspaper is seen folded and spread out, fruit is sliced up, clothes are ironed and folded. Much of this learning is visual and the experiences incidental. Without effective vision, access to these experiences will be severely reduced.

These are, then, the three main factors to consider in establishing the special needs of children with visual impairments:

1. Without the use of the coordinating sense of vision, exploration will be through sequential experiences which have to be synthesized into a whole. This is complex and takes more time than normal visual exploration.
2. The features and characteristics which are of help and interest to a child exploring tactually may be different from those which are important to the sighted child.
3. The quantity and quality of experiences will be restricted and this, in particular, will make incidental learning difficult.

Lowenfeld (1950) examined the effects of blindness on development and came to similar conclusions. He expressed them succinctly as three basic limitations. A blind child would be limited:

1. in the range and variety of his experiences;
2. in his ability to get about;
3. in his interaction with the environment.

Conclusion

From all these factors it is possible to identify two common elements and suggest that, although an over-simplification which does not bear close examination, they are useful *aides-mémoires* to summarize this section. The special needs of children with a visual impairment are based on two areas of difficulty:

• understanding relationships;
• gaining stimulation from the environment.

The former area may result in delayed cognitive development, mobility and orientation difficulties and problems gaining reassurance about one's actions or events in the environment. The latter area may affect the ability to learn through incidental experiences and result in restricted experiences and misunderstanding.

One of the roles of parents and educators is to help their children overcome these effects of visual handicap by enabling them to gain access to the experiences they need. They will need:

- more information;
- more accurate information;
- more structured information;
- more time to assimilate information.

We will go on to examine the ways in which this can be achieved in subsequent chapters.

Summary

1. Definitions of blindness and partial sight are usually based on medical criteria which differ from a layman's understanding of these terms.
2. The process of seeing involves both the reception of signals in the eye and the interpretation of these signals by the brain.
3. The effects of eye defects are varied and result in the need for different viewing conditions.
4. Vision is a major sense for learning and lack of complete vision can affect learning in several ways.

CHAPTER 2

Population and History

The Population

Who are the children with a visual impairment? How many should we expect to find in a given population? Are the number and type of children changing? What additional handicaps occur with a visual impairment? An overview of this information is presented here as it will be of general interest. It should help readers put their own children into a wider perspective. It may help teachers to anticipate the sort of children they can expect to work with in the field of visual impairment. Those who need more detailed data, such as staff responsible for planning services, may find it helpful to study the Royal National Institute for the Blind (RNIB) Demographic Studies (1985a, b and c) which provide a comprehensive review of data on numbers and the demographic characteristics of the visually disabled population.

Prevalence

In the age range 5–15, the prevalence rate of about 3 blind children per 10,000 children can be expected and about 4.2 partially sighted children per 10,000. These figures can be extrapolated from Department of Health (DOH) figures for registered blind and partially sighted people and RNIB estimates of under-registration in this age group. However, considerable caution must be attached to this over-simplified statistic.

The Department of Education and Science (DES) in their figures for

1982 give a prevalence of 1.16 per 10,000 for blind children and 2.43 per 10,000 for partially sighted children. Why might there be this discrepancy and how accurate are the figures?

One difficulty is that many statistics are based on registration and not all children with visual impairment are registered. This procedure is carried out by social services departments and is generally dependent on visual acuity. A certificate of registration, called Form BD8, must be signed by a qualified ophthalmic specialist. Registration will give the patient access to certain services and benefits (see Klemtz 1977; Ford 1986) although most educational services do not require registration before they can become involved.

In the pre-school years, children with total blindness or very severe visual impairment are likely to be identified and registered without much difficulty. Indeed, in the pre-school age range, the number of registered totally blind children always exceeds the number of partially sighted (1981: 260 as against 160), although the reverse obtained by the age of 9. Those with less severe impairments may not yet be displaying learning difficulties or a visual impairment may not be suspected. Therefore the pre-school number will not include a large number of children with poor vision who have not been identified as visually impaired. Another group of children who are unlikely to be registered at this stage are the multi-handicapped children with a visual impairment. This may be because of difficulty in assessing visual acuity or because it is not thought worthwhile to embark on the procedure as the benefits are marginal for this group. A third group which might be excluded are those children who have been identified but whose parents prefer them not to be registered as blind or whose assessment or prognosis is uncertain and so registration is delayed.

For the school-age years, it is likely that most totally blind children and those with very poor vision will be included in figures for registration. There may still be a significant number of additionally or multiple handicapped children who have not been assessed or included in the figures. The number of partially sighted children referred for special education tends to peak at ages 8–9 as it is then that educational difficulties become so apparent that the children need some special treatment. This, in turn, may result in registration, although a smaller percentage of partially sighted people are registered than of blind as the benefits are very much less. RNIB (1985b) calculated that the true prevalence figure for partial sight is about 85 per cent higher than the figure from registration. Of course, as stated earlier, not all children who receive educational support from services for the visually impaired will be registered as blind or partially sighted. This latter point is particularly important if services are planned on the basis of registration figures.

No large-scale study has been carried out on the prevalence of visual impairment in children. Studies of adults, for example by Cullinan (1977), clearly indicate that the registers are not full records of people with visual impairment. Cullinan, reviewing a number of studies, found that only about 51 per cent of adults with a significant sight loss were registered. An RNIB report (1985b) examined a wide range of factors that might affect the child population and concluded that the registration figures probably under-estimated the population of children by 25 per cent.

The DES base their figures on visually impaired children receiving or awaiting entry into special education. This depends on returns from schools and local education authorities (LEAs) in which the children are identified as visually impaired. It is likely that a number of children, particularly those with multiple handicaps, will not be listed in these returns, especially when visual impairment is not seen as the major handicap. The author has personal correspondence with a number of peripatetic teachers of the visually impaired who have established new services. This consistently shows that LEA lists under-estimate the number of children by at least 100 per cent. A major factor which affects the estimates are the different criteria used to establish visual impairment. The educationist will be identifying children who seem to have significant difficulty in carrying out school work because of visual problems. The registration figures are likely to be based on an acuity score. Head teachers may base their returns on children who are receiving specialist services. Finally, it should be pointed out that the children form a very small part of the total population of people with visual impairments. Over 75 per cent of the visually impaired population is over 65 years of age and the prevalence rate is about 120 per 10,000 as opposed to 3 per 10,000 for children.

Trends

The figures for registered blind and partially sighted children might be most helpful in examining the changes in numbers of children with visual impairment over a period of years (see Table 2.1).

Table 2.1 Registered children 0–15 in England and Wales (DHSS)

	1960	*1970*	*1982*
Blind	2272	2113	2079
Partially sighted	2292	2739	2319

The figures for blind children have shown a small but steady decline for over twenty years. Amongst reasons for this are developments in medical treatment of children born with defects, preventative medicine to eradicate the causes of blindness, improved genetic counselling and termination of severely handicapped foetuses. The decline is not so marked for partially sighted children. Awareness of partial sightedness may have increased and resulted in more children being registered. While causes of blindness are being eradicated, causes of poor vision, often occurring with other handicaps, have been increasing. Projections for the future, calculated by taking into account changes in population and medical developments, show that the population of children with visual impairments is not expected to change, in absolute terms, very much over the next twenty years (see Table 2.2).

Table 2.2 Projections of visually impaired children in England and Wales RNIB (1985b)

	1981	1991	2001
Blind	2210	9179	2228
Partially sighted	2605	2300	2664

What does need to be examined are the causes of impairments and the type of child who will make up the population.

Data is not collected, so as to be readily accessible, on the causes of impairment and the presence of other impairments in children with a visual impairment. The visual impairments may be described on form BD8 but the cause of these impairments (epidemiology) is often unknown. Hereditary defects form the single largest groups, with other congenital abnormalities making these congenital defects responsible for up to 60 per cent of visual impairments (Warburg 1986). DHSS (the then Department of Health and Social Security) statistics for the causes of blindness and partial sight in children for the period 1976–85 (Bulletin 5/86) show the main cause of blindness to be optic atrophy (30 per cent of total). Retinal conditions, such as retrolental fibroplasia (ROP) and retinal dystrophies account for about 20 per cent of the total. Cataracts and other congenital abnormalities such as buphthalmos, microphthalmos and coloboma account for another 20 per cent. Causes of partial sight are somewhat similar with optic atrophy as a major cause. However, nystagmus is given as the main cause of partial sight (18 per cent of the total). Cataracts (14 per cent) and other congenital abnormalities together make up about 27 per cent of the total number.

Although the causes have remained fairly constant over the ten-year period, between 1980 and 1986 a number of babies were born with ROP. This defect, caused by giving excess oxygen to premature babies, had been a major cause of blindness in the 1950s. After the dangers of this life-saving treatment were identified, a number of ROP children dropped dramatically. If we are to see a re-emergence of this as a significant cause of blindness during the 1980s, it may reflect medical efforts to use technology to give life to infants of extremely low birth rate. ROP is rare in babies over 1,000-gm birth weight. Many causes of visual impairments which were common earlier this century have now been controlled if not eradicated, for example syphilis, meningitis, rubella, diabetes, toxocara canis and vitamin deficiencies. A few children were born blind as a result of their mothers taking thalidomide. The unexplained birth defects are very often associated with other handicaps and the population of children born with multiple handicaps has increased considerably over the past twenty years.

The Vernon Report (Vernon 1972: 9) stated that 'The total proportion of blind children with any additional handicap (between the ages of 5 and 15 years) rose from 39% in 1959 to 50.6% in 1970.' Although similar data was not available for partially sighted children, the report stated that over 23 per cent suffered from additional handicaps. 'We believe that among the partially sighted as well as among the blind, the prevalence of additional handicaps is an increasing problem (p. 9).' This belief has certainly been proved true by subsequent figures. Colborne-Brown and Tobin (1982), in a postal questionnaire of families with a registered blind child, found 74 per cent of the sample to be multi-handicapped; 47 per cent of the sample had a mental handicap in addition to the visual impairment. RNIB (1985c) estimated that probably 87 per cent of all blind and 66 per cent of partially sighted children had other handicaps. Colborne-Brown points out that many of these children are currently outside the provision for the visually handicapped and, in the past, could well have been left out of figures of services for visually handicapped children. The RNIB report goes a step further and, from detailed examination of all available sources, suggests that there are at least as many severely mentally retarded children who are registrably blind as there are already registered (about 1,500) and a similar number of partially sighted children. The majority of children who are visually impaired are, then, additionally handicapped. What other difficulties are they likely to have?

Studies by Griffiths (1979), Warburg *et al.* (1979), Colborne-Brown and Tobin (1982), Best (1983), Ellis (1986), as well as statistics from the DHSS, provide a mass of information about the likelihood of other impairments occurring with visual impairment. However, the different bases and criteria used in these studies make it impossible to simplify the information into a table of incidence of each of the various additional impairments. This task, attempted by Moss in the RNIB study on demography, resulted in a 70-page report. It is possible to extract some crude generalizations from the figures which give some indication of the likely composition of the population.

The largest group of children would seem to be those with severe mental handicaps and multi-handicaps. They probably form at least 50 per cent of the total number of visually handicapped children. Within this group will be several hundred children who have been identified as deaf-blind. The next largest group will be those with physical impairments and a figure of 10–20 per cent of the population of visually handicapped children could be justified from a study of the various studies. Other sub-groups include children with emotional and behavioural difficulties and children with moderate learning difficulties. Figures are even more vague for these groups but, together, they probably constitute about 10 per cent of the total population. Almost all other known conditions are also found with visual impairments – physical deformities, growth deficiencies, epilepsy, heart disease, speech defects, psychiatric disturbances.

The concept of special educational needs embodied in the Education Act, 1981, which should have replaced the idea of a single major handicap, is particularly appropriate for many of these children. However, the problems that are raised relate to the services which can meet these needs. With such a range of impairments in so many combinations, how can appropriate expertise be made available to meet the needs? The solution, of course, is multi-disciplinary team-work in which the peripatetic teacher of the visually impaired has an important role, as do the schools for the visually impaired. We will describe the development of services and then, in the next chapter, examine the range of services currently available to help these children and their families.

History of Services

Louis Braille was blinded shortly after his third birthday. He had an accident in his father's blacksmith's workshop. By the time he was 20, in 1829, Louis had already realized that the key to his success as a blind man was access to print material. In particular, he was a musician and needed a way of reading and writing music. This required an effective system to replace the cumbersome raised letters that were used in the very few available books. When Louis Braille first went to the school for the blind in Paris, there were just three books in the library. By the age of 30 he had perfected his code, abandoning the previous concept of raising print shapes and using a pattern of dots. He devised seven basic characters, probably one for each note in the music scale, and arranged these into four rows adding dots to represent notes of different length. According to some historians, by a happy coincidence this also gave enough characters for letters of the alphabet and some punctuation. He then extended the number of characters to allow for common combinations of letters, which became some of the contractions we use today. The code appalled many sighted people who felt it would isolate the blind from the 'real' world and, perhaps, also would involve them in the extra trouble of learning it. But it delighted many blind people who realized the fluency and speed that could be achieved with a system designed for finger reading. Braille died of pulmonary consumption in 1852, at the age of 43, while the debate about his system was still raging. It would be another 40 years before the system was accepted in the UK and a hundred years before he was officially recognized as a national hero in France. In 1952, on the hundredth anniversary of his death, his body was removed from the village graveyard in Coupvrey and reinterred in the Panthéon in Paris. In recognition, though, of his enormous contribution to making the hand into the eyes of the blind, his hands were cut off and left in their original resting place.

Braille was one of a series of pioneers, many of them blind, who influenced society's attitude to blind people and were responsible for developing educational services and opportunities for the blind.

Throughout history, blind people have often been imbued with an aura of mysticism. The blind soothsayer in *Julius Caesar* had 'inner vision'. Blind people in China and India were often employed as storytellers because of their apparently outstanding memories, due, it was assumed, to the lack of visual distraction to fill their minds. Charlboix, (cited in Guillie 1918: 22) in his history of Japan, records that:

> The annals of the empire, the histories of great men or the ancient deeds of families, are not more certain documents than the memory of these illustrious blind men who, communicating their knowledge to each other, form an historical tradition which nobody pretends to contradict.

But blindness itself, as opposed to blind people, has often been seen as a sign of evil. Plato supports, in his writing, the Spartan practice of leaving blind children to die on the hillside. Oedipus was blinded for looking at his naked mother. Even until recently in the UK superstitions often linked incest with the birth of a blind baby. It is far from unknown, in parts of West Africa, for a blind infant to be left under a banana tree for days so that the evil spirits may take him back. Services and attitudes, though, have generally improved and significant developments took place during the nineteenth century.

By the beginning of that century a great deal was already known about blindness and ways of helping blind people. In 1773, Diderot in his *Essay on Blindness* observed:

> The difficulty which blind persons have in finding things mislaid makes them love regularity and exactness; and I have observed that those about them imbibe the quality, whether from good example set by the blind, or from a human concern for them. (p. 70)

He recounts the conversation in which a blind man, asked if he would be glad to have his sight restored, replied:

> If it were not for curiosity, I would just as soon have long arms; it seems to me my hands would tell me more of what goes on in the moon than your eyes or your telescopes; and besides, eyes cease to see sooner than hands to touch. I would be as well off if I perfected the organs I possess, as if I obtained the organ which I am deprived of. (p. 77)

The concept of developing the use of residual senses was emerging, although this would turn into the fallacy that the release of energy that sighted people consume using their eyes could result in heightened ability in the other senses.

Guillie, Director of the Institute for the Blind in Paris, published his *Instructions and Amusements for the Blind* in 1819. This contains assertions, many of which could today be supported by research evidence.

> The Teacher will never succeed, unless he is thoroughly persuaded that the blind perceive things quite differently from us; that they do not attach the same ideas to words. . . . (p. 2)

> We do not sufficiently consider that the blind, who can only have successive ideas of the objects which he touches, must necessarily at first form different opinions of things, which, though identical in their form, differ in size. (p. 73)

Therefore some knowledge was there, although services were in their infancy. In 1786 the first institution for the education of the blind in Europe was founded in Paris. Valentin Huey, one of the greatest pioneering educators of the blind and founder of the Paris institute, wrote an essay in the same year in which he states his concern for the 'sad condition of his sightless countrymen'. He describes an incident that had affected the direction of his life. He noted a 'novelty entertainment' taking place in a café:

> Eight to ten poor blind persons, with spectacles on their noses, placed along a desk which sustained instruments of music, where they executed a discordant symphony, seemed to give delight to the audience. A very different sentiment possessed our soul, and we conceived, at that very instant, the possibility of realising, to the advantage of those unfortunate

people, the means of which they had only an apparent and ridiculous
enjoyment. . . . Do they not know objects by the diversity of their forms?
. . . Why can they not distinguish an A from a B in orthography?

This could well have been the beginning of systematic education for the
blind that, two hundred years later, we accept as commonplace.

The first school of instruction in the UK was started, just a few years
after the Paris institution, in Liverpool in 1790. It was called an asylum
and the object was 'to render the blind happy in themselves and useful
to society'. This was followed in the next three years by the establishment
of asylums in Edinburgh and Bristol. Throughout the nineteenth century
the arguments about reading type continued to dominate the interest of
many educators. Services continued to develop for children and adults,
although there was little coordination in their growth. The founding of
the Royal Victoria School in Newcastle, for example, was decided upon
by the city council as the best way to celebrate the coronation of Queen
Victoria. After lengthy debate 'it was decided that instead of an illumination of the town, a subscription should be raised and applied to the
erection of a building to be entitled "The Royal Victoria Asylum for the
Blind".' The aims of the asylum were 'to offer to the indigent blind a
religious, moral and elementary education founded on Scriptural principles and to teach them such trades as are suitable to their capacities'
(Phillips 1938).

In 1860, a 36-year-old doctor, Thomas Armitage, had to give up his
medical practice in London due to failing eyesight. Over the next thirty
years he was to make a most significant change in the provision of services to blind people throughout the UK. Illingworth (1910: p. 92) in his
History of Education of the Blind describes Armitage's reaction to his
blindness:

> This blind world, Dr. Armitage soon found, was anything but a beautiful
> place, and, characteristically, he began his attempts to improve it with that
> class whose loss was the most deplorable of all, viz. the indigent blind of
> London. He joined the Committee of the Indigent Blind Visiting Society,
> which, although it had been in existence for five-and-twenty years, had
> not, up to that time answered the expectations of its founders. In 1865 Dr.
> Armitage persuaded the committee to appoint a blind man as one of their
> visitors. This departure proved a great success, and vacancies as they
> occurred were filled up in a similar manner; and now the society's visitors
> are all chosen from the blind.

He quickly realized the chaos that was being created by the debate over
the types used for reading and writing and also became convinced that
many of the difficulties in education of the blind were caused by sighted
managers and teachers who did not understand the problems faced by the

blind nor the best ways of overcoming them. In 1868 Armitage founded the British and Foreign Blind Association and his first activity was to examine, with other blind men, the different types for reading and writing. They decided the Braille system was the best and successfully set about influencing all establishments to adopt its use, a phenomenal achievement, given the strength of feeling amongst interested parties. His influence was paramount in giving direction to services and in enabling new institutions to develop. He brought about the founding of the Royal Normal College of Music for the Blind (now the Royal National College) to help prepare young people for gainful employment, particularly in music. He initiated a Royal Commission into the education of the blind which led, in 1893, to an education bill making compulsory the education of all blind children between the ages of 6 and 16. This Association grew and, eventually, became the Royal National Institute for the Blind. Armitage died in 1890, a few days after being thrown from his horse, but his energy and, metaphorically, clear-sightedness influenced services in the UK for a long time.

By 1910 there were at least thirty schools for the blind, mostly residential, and the teachers in those schools were now required by the Board of Education to obtain a specialist teaching qualification issued by the newly formed College of Teachers of the Blind. Although the issue of the reading medium had been largely settled and the curriculum had been examined critically, particularly with regard to physical health and exercise, the issue of whether blind teachers should teach blind children was in full debate. Blind people were becoming centrally involved in organizing and managing many other services and it was seen as a logical employment for school leavers. As standards became more rigorous, though, doubts were expressed about the wisdom of this practice continuing. Protagonists pointed out that a blind person could probably excel at teaching braille, arithmetic and music and 'as a rule, give over more of his leisure time to thinking over and preparing lessons for schools than could reasonably be expected of his seeing colleague' (Illingworth 1910). They could be an incentive and encouragement to the pupils. The practical arrangements for supervising their work was described by Illingworth:

> In Britain, many of the blind schools have now adopted the class-room system, one class being separated from another by a glazed partition, so that the Principal can direct supervision over the whole. By this system, also, two blind teachers and three seeing make an excellent staff for five classes, the seeing teacher being able to call his blind colleague's attention to any misconduct or eccentric movement on the part of any member of his class. Such an arrangement has proved very successful in many British schools. (p. 163)

By 1936, a survey on the education of blind children carried out by the College of Teachers of the Blind, concluded that:

> It is generally admitted that blind teachers have a special understanding of, and sympathy with blind children . . . they can give advice out of their own experience . . . they provide a valuable source of inspiration . . . but it would be absurd to contend they have not their limitations. They cannot, for instance, take as full a share in many outdoor games and physical activities as their seeing colleagues, nor are they able, with equal facility, to correct the mannerisms to which young children are so prone. For this latter reason, we do not think it would be in the best interest of the children for a blind teacher to have sole responsibility for an infant school or for a class of junior children, although in some parts of the work of children of this age, such as handicrafts, braille reading and writing, they are capable of doing most efficient work. (p. 17)

In that 1936 report, the number of schools for the blind was listed as 34 with a total of just over 2,000 children. Just over 4,000 children were classified as partially sighted with about one-third of this number attending local schools. In 1931, for the first time, statistics had been collected on the number of children using braille and print and at that time slightly less than one-half the children in schools for the blind were recorded as being taught braille. Although the concept of the enhancement of residual vision had not yet been formulated, there was an awareness of the presence of residual vision in many blind children.

The report examines curriculum in detail and describes modified teaching approaches. Many issues will be familiar to today's teachers. For example, in 1936, the practice of introducing braille to children was through an uncontracted code having one-to-one correspondence with print. The report draws attention to experimental work in the School for the Blind at Swiss Cottage and in America which used 'Grade 2' braille which contained contracted and abbreviated words with extra signs for common letter combination: 'The teaching of contractions to beginning braille readers promotes greater speed of reading and in some cases greater accuracy . . . no adverse effect on spelling was observed.' The report commends this approach for consideration. Since the 1950s, it has been the standard approach and only in the mid-1980s has it been seriously challenged again, starting up a virtual re-run of the earlier debate. This time, though, there is a firmer basis of research into reading to help the discussion. There is also a significant change in the abilities of the children, due to the presence of many additional handicaps.

Teachers are encouraged to examine the teaching of arithmetic carefully and to keep a true sense of proportion in the amount of time spent on this in relation to the needs of the blind:

It will be sufficient if blind children can be taught to understand notation and the simple arithmetical processes. This is much more important than that they should be skilled in working out long multiplication or division sums or other more complicated problems. Such a skill is largely worthless and can only be obtained at the sacrifice of valuable time.

The importance of sex education was recognized and the authors state that for the teachers of the blind children:

> We should like to see, as an integral part of their training, a course in Sex Instruction which would enable them to meet sex situations and even crude questions with sympathetic understanding and without flinching.

They recognized that, for the children, many sources of knowledge are closed and 'touch as a conveyor of sex knowledge is, however, liable to cause far greater psychological disturbance than sight. While statuettes and models have their value, it is easy to overestimate this.'

A major issue raised by the report for the first time is that of integration. In the early 1900s this had already been debated in the USA and many public-school programmes enrolled partially seeing and blind children. In the UK, the vast majority of blind children still attended special schools. The arguments in this 1936 report would be very familiar to readers of post-Warnock literature:

> What, then, are the educational advantages claimed for the system?
> 1. The advantage of the blind child remaining in his home environment.
> 2. The social and educational advantages of the blind child being brought into contact with fully sighted children in the ordinary Elementary School.

The report's conclusions are that the special needs of braille readers and their preparation for specialist vocations will not be adequately met in the ordinary schools, although they do recognize the advantages of partially seeing children being educated in special classes in ordinary schools.

> We are of the opinion that the education of blind children, particularly of young blind children, is of too specialised a character to permit its being treated as an appendage to the scheme of education in the ordinary elementary school. In forming that conclusion, however, it should be understood that the committee has in mind the blind child of average attainment. The conclusion must not be construed as definitely closing against the gifted blind child all other avenues than the present type of school for the blind.

While these developments had been taking place in the education of the blind, the education of partially sighted children had evolved along separate lines. At the turn of the century a partially sighted child might attend an ordinary school or a school for the blind. By 1907, a Board of

Education report had recommended that these 'weak-sighted' children should be taught by visual methods and that special classes in ordinary schools be established for them. But it was thought that some children, particularly the 'myopes', could be harmed by the use of their vision and therefore restrictions were placed on these visual methods. A child would not be allowed to undertake fine work, such as art and handicrafts; he would have very limited participation in games and physical education; length of time spent reading and writing was carefully controlled; oral work took up a large part of the school day. These classes became known as 'sight-saving classes'. In a brief survey of the history of education of the partially sighted, Sister Kathleen Fothergill (1980) wrote:

> The restrictions imposed, based on the principles that sight must be saved, and that over-use and close work were responsible for eye strain, were to hamper developments in the education of the partially sighted for many years to come. (p. 12)

Subsequently a wide range of educational approaches developed in these classes and the schools for the blind. The restrictions on the use of vision were questioned by some teachers and ophthalmologists. A 1934 Board of Education committee reported on the current wide range of approaches. It took ophthalmological advice, looked at the achievements of the children and recommended that the restrictions on close work should be relaxed. Partially sighted children were no longer to be educated in schools for the blind but in classes in ordinary schools or in newly created schools for the partially sighted. Teachers experimented with methods of using whatever degree of sight a child possessed. A revolution in methods was taking place and this reversal of accepted practice caused much debate amongst experienced teachers.

By 1972 the Vernon Report on Education of the Visually Handicapped (a new term coined in the USA and the subject of much derision and objection in letter columns of journals at the time) recommended that 'Para. 11.28: blind and partially sighted children would benefit from being educated in the same schools, though need to be in separate classes at the junior stage.' However, opinion was still split and of sixty-four recommendations this was the only one which was not endorsed by all members of the committee (two members dissented). The report also recommended the increased use of low-vision aids and adjustable lighting.

The same year, in Texas, the mother of a partially sighted girl was encouraging her daughter to use these aids but was also trying to find other methods of helping her daughter to see better. As a lecturer in special education, she turned to training programmes rather than mechanical aids and found that a series of training exercises seemed to help her daughter make better use of her remaining vision. The mother, Natalie Barraga, developed this into an assessment and training procedure. Within the space of five years, her ideas had become an integral part of the philosophy of education of partially sighted children in the USA. This concept of the development of visual efficiency through systematic training in the use of residual vision led to the development of the Look and Think material at the University of Birmingham in England and, subsequently, its adoption as a central tenet of educational philosophy in the UK.

Educational services for the blind and partially sighted were being brought together again, although some teaching approaches were different and based on a clearer understanding of children's needs than ever before. Throughout the 1970s the concept of need rather than categories of handicap was increasingly used in determining the most appropriate placement for children. This resulted in the present range of services which are described in the next chapter.

Summary

The population of children with visual impairments has changed dramatically over the past twenty years with an increase in the number of children with multiple handicaps and a decrease in the proportion of totally blind children. After many years of separate education, services for all children with visual impairments have now come together with both partially sighted and totally blind children now taught in the same schools. Educational philosophy has also evolved, further blurring the distinction between these two groups of children, with many children now given training in developing the efficient use of any remaining vision they may possess.

children during their school years. The educational services will therefore be keen to become involved at the earliest opportunity.

The peripatetic teacher of the visually impaired is likely to have an important role in helping the child directly and in guiding the family to provide appropriate stimulation. The teacher's skill in educational counselling will include explaining the effects of the visual defect on the child's vision and, if necessary, offering an explanation of the defect itself. The latter task will not be needed if the parents have been able to take in the information given to them by an ophthalmologist or member of his staff. Very often, though, lack of time in the clinic, emotional upset and the need for time to digest the facts, results in the specialist teacher being the professional who is asked questions on this topic. The information will be given from an educational, not medical, background and will concentrate on the condition and its effects on the child's vision rather than on aspects of cause, treatment and prognosis.

The teacher may also be responsible for offering parents or care-givers suggestions on management and stimulation. This will require an assessment of the child's performance to determine strengths and weaknesses in order to draw up suggestions for intervention. The teacher will use a knowledge of child development and the development of children with visual impairments in order to structure observations which are necessary to gain information about the child's performance. Many teachers will want to structure their observations further by reference to a published developmental scale such as the Reynell-Zinkin Scale (Reynell and Zinkin 1979), the Oregon Project (Brown *et al.* 1991) or 'Reach out and teach' (Ferrell 1980). The latter two materials contain suggestions for intervention in addition to assessment scales. All these scales suggest significant milestones in a child's development in different areas of activity – for example, language, self-care, movement. Information on the child's performance can be obtained through talking with parents and others familiar with the child. Open-ended questions such as 'What happens at bath time?' are likely to produce useful information which can be followed up with further questioning, observation or a specially constructed activity. The use of very specific questions, such as are found on assessment forms (e.g. 'Can he hold a cup?', 'Does he stand without support?'), may also be appropriate. In this case, the parent and teacher together can sort out what the child can do. They will need to examine the criteria required of each item and establish if the child has the skill required by the item. There is a choice of four decisions for each item. That the child has the skill (or has developed beyond the stage when it is appropriate, e.g. babbling when the child can talk); that the child does not have the skill; that the skill is emerging but not established; that there has been no opportunity for the child to develop the skill. In this last case and when there is uncertainty about the child's skill, the parents can collect more information by trying out specific activities with the child. The teacher and parent can then – again together – set goals for future achievements. Scales for use with children who have visual impairments should cover all major areas of development including movement and mobility, the use of touch and hands for exploration, the development of residual vision. Information on appropriate scales and their use can be found in Best (1987b; 1988). Some pre-school support services are organized so that the teacher can work directly with the child on a frequent (e.g. weekly) basis. This requires a small case-load of perhaps fifteen to twenty if the support is to be continued over a period of months and it is desirable for the teacher to have had experience of working with this age range. This model is used in parts of the USA, Australia and some European countries. However, in the UK, it is more common for case-loads to be very much in excess of this and therefore support teachers have to act as advisers to parents and other care-givers rather than work directly with the child. The child may attend a play group, child development centre or nursery school, and parents may receive visits from a pre-school teacher of the handicapped. These are the kind of services and people that the specialist teacher will need to work with to ensure the child and family receive a coordinated programme of stimulation and advice.

Many, but not all, LEAs have a peripatetic specialist teacher or service for the visually impaired. Where such a person has not been appointed, the LEA can call on the Education Advisory Service of the RNIB. This service consists of a team of experienced teachers who will visit the child at the invitation of the local authority and offer advice and suggestions for intervention.

There are a number of specialist classes and schools for children in this age range. Many schools for the visually handicapped (in 1986 there were twenty-six in England and Wales) take children of nursery age and provide day educational facilities for them. This would be in a separate class or unit to the main school but teachers would have access to the equipment and expertise available in the school. Thirteen of the schools have residential facilities which are generally used by nursery-age children in exceptional circumstances. There is, however, a constant demand for residential places for children under the age of 5 and the RNIB runs three residential nursery schools. These offer specialist teaching in a small setting and can be of particular help to children with complex handicaps and families who need to have the handicapped child placed away from home.

School-age Provision

By the end of the 1980s, there were probably as many children with visual impairments in special schools for the visually impaired as in other placements. DES figures for 1982 indicate that 90 per cent of blind children and 75 per cent of partially sighted children (who had no other major handicap) were in special schools for the visually handicapped. It was suggested that, by the end of the decade, at least 10 per cent of blind children and 50 per cent of partially sighted children would be educated in ordinary schools in special units. The move to place the majority of children in ordinary schools received an enormous boost, of course, with the Education Act, 1981, and DES projections probably under-estimate the proportion of children now integrated. Subsequent to this act, there has been a rapid increase in the number of peripatetic teachers of the visually impaired appointed throughout the country. What range of services is now available? What can each service offer? What factors might determine the most appropriate placement for a child?

Special Schools

There are about thirty residential and day schools for the visually impaired throughout the UK. The majority of residential schools are non-maintained and run by independent organizations, while most of the day schools are run by LEAs. The residential schools continue to provide accommodation for those children whose special needs, or whose parents, require it. These children may be multi-handicapped and need the very special expertise of a multi-disciplinary staff with a 24-hour learning programme; they may be children losing their sight who need a period of time in a very supportive environment with intensive teaching of new skills in independence and learning; they may be children whose parents, for many different reasons, have great difficulty in coping with the children in their home at least at some stage in the child's school life. Some parents prefer their child to grow up and learn in a special-school environment, believing that the small classes and specialist teachers are more appropriate for the child's personality, learning style or ability than the facilities of a mainstream school.

Most of the residential special schools have a regional intake and provide weekly boarding facilities. Some are also developing particular expertise in meeting the needs of sub-groups of children, as is described later in this chapter, and so become a national focus for services. These services are changing rapidly. For example, out of a total of about twenty schools, between 1985 and 1990 three schools closed down, two changed the type of children they accepted, three added new departments. This pattern continues to evolve in response to changing needs brought about by changes in the child population and in the development of complementary services in the mainstream sector.

Nearly all the schools, whether originally for blind or partially sighted children, now take both braille and printed readers. They feature small classes, usually four to five blind children and no more than twelve children when print readers. Teaching approaches will be adapted to suit the needs of the children and the curriculum is likely to be modified to include the special areas required by many children, for example, development in residual vision, mobility and independent living skills. Within the framework of the National Curriculum, the balance may also be altered to allow sufficient time and emphasis on critical areas such as listening skills, experience through visits and fluency in reading.

Many of the schools now have children who have problems in addition to a visual impairment. They have responded to this need by appointing ancillary staff from various disciplines who work as part of a teaching team. This may include a psychologist, speech therapist, physiotherapist, mobility instructor, teacher of the deaf as well as classroom aides. The schools have a range of specialist equipment, not only in the area of visual impairment (magnifier, closed-circuit television, braille duplicator, talking computer terminals, etc.) but in these other areas. All teachers of classes of children with visual impairments have a DES mandatory requirement to have specialist training in education of the visually handicapped. The schools still provide a full-time education for most of the children but other services are being developed. Some schools have an 'out reach' service with a member of staff visiting non-specialist schools to give advice on teaching a child with a visual impairment. This is usually an appointment additional to the school's teaching staff, although sometimes a member of the school staff will become involved because advice is sought in a specialist curriculum area. Many schools offer assessment placements. These may be for several weeks and will allow the child time to settle in and the staff the opportunity to collect information through teaching. The outcome of these placements will be an identification of the child's educational needs and suggestions for the placement and teaching of the child.

In the future, it is likely that schools will change considerably in their role. This certainly is the experience of many other countries and of other branches of special education in this country. The DES, in 1984, drew up proposals for the future provision for visually handicapped pupils in special schools. This envisaged a continuing need for special schools but recommended that secondary schools should have no less than 80 pupils and primary schools no less than 30. This, the report stated, was necessary to ensure that the curriculum could match up to what is offered in ordinary schools. Wherever possible, the primary and secondary provision should be separate. The total number of school places available in 1984 exceeded the need and this would continue into the 1990s unless there were a rationalization of the provision. This meant the closure of a number of schools.

The services offered by the schools may well change in the future. An important feature of healthy schools will be their willingness to cooperate with the services integrating children. They may, for example, be able to offer specialist assessment facilities using materials and expertise that is not readily available in every local area. They could offer short-term placements for children who are integrated, perhaps on an annual residential basis, in which there is the opportunity to meet other visually handicapped children and also to receive intensive training in areas not fully covered by the integrated programme, perhaps in faster braille reading, independent living skills, social skills and use of technology or mobility. These courses may be offered during traditional school holidays. Children who lose their vision during school years are often particularly vulnerable in the few months following the onset of blindness. The trauma of loss and lack of skills can cause severe emotional and educational problems which can often be helped by the special-school environment. Both residential and day schools have a good record of helping children and parents in this difficult period and this could continue to be an important role for schools in the future. The schools could offer a service in the preparation of materials by modifying and enlarging text and the use of graphic materials and tape-recording. They may be involved in personnel training and staff development by arranging meetings, workshops and courses for staff and parents. By being part of a regional service, or even at the hub of the service, they may well be an indispensable part of future provision.

Two other factors may affect the role of special schools in the future. Visual impairment is a very low-incidence handicap and this creates particular difficulties in providing for children in rural areas. One solution to this difficulty is to use a residential-school placement and this may continue to be a role for these schools. A second fact may be the increasing proportion of multi-handicapped children within the population of children with visual impairments. The special school may be seen as the best place to meet all the educational needs of these children. In particular, the residential schools would be able to provide a 24-hour programme of specialist training and stimulation and, perhaps, all-year care not just for a traditional three school terms. Since Warnock, it seems to have been increasingly assumed that parents are able and want, or should want, to cope with their handicapped child in the home. This has made it unfashionable for parents to seek residential provision as a way of meeting the enormous demands made by the presence of a multi-handicapped child in some families. If this fashion were to change, there may be a continued role for special schools. Whether residential schools for the visually impaired are seen to be able to fulfil this role is a second consideration. They will have to provide the full range of professional expertise and curriculum required so that all a child's needs are met by the school. There will also have to be an appreciation amongst special educational administrators who arrange placements that visual impairment can have a central and critical effect on learning and therefore placement in a centre where this is fully understood is the most appropriate placement. The development of this understanding may need some active promotion by the services for the visually impaired, if they are to take on this role with multi-handicapped children as a major part of their work in the future.

Integrated Provision

Services for children in mainstream schools can be divided broadly into those which provide a specialist teacher in the school and those which offer peripatetic services of support, advice or teaching.

The school-based services usually take the form of a resource room used by the specialist teacher and, on occasions, by the children. Alternatively a unit facility may be provided in which the children and teacher are based. The resource-room provision seems to be most favoured as it allows the children to be registered in a mainstream class with a child receiving support in this class with his peers. The resource room may be used for teaching specialist subjects, preparation of material, individual study by children, and for the storage of equipment and books. The unit will be more a base for teaching children, with individuals joining in mainstream classes at selected times and the teacher spending most of her time with a group of children in a unit room.

In both cases teachers will have similar decisions to make about the range of equipment needed and the organization of the timetable. The range of equipment will depend on the age and visual state of the children. There is likely to be a number of low-vision aids, desk lights, closed-circuit televisions, large-print typewriters, bright and coloured writing paper – some with heavy lines – several types of pen and pencils, speeded speech tape-recorders with study and recreational material on cassettes. If there are braille readers, there will be braille writing and duplicating equipment, braille text books, computers for the production of braille and print texts, maths equipment, diagram and map-making apparatus. There may be an enlarging photocopier if the school machine is not used. The teacher is likely to build up an extensive collection of catalogues and names of suppliers of appropriate equipment and services as well as details of the children, their medical condition, taxi/telephone numbers, and so on. A reference library of books may also be kept in the resource room or unit, although some teachers prefer to keep these in a general staff collection to encourage other teachers to notice them.

Decisions about the timetable will be made with the main school staff, and these present greater difficulties. The aim of the service will be to provide a balanced curriculum for each child and this often involves a selection from the curriculum in order to allow sufficient time for adequate coverage of required core areas as well as the inclusion of specialist areas in the timetable. Practical subjects and physical education are often considered easiest to drop as they present most difficulty for both teacher and child, but it must be recognized that the resulting timetable may exclude the child from important educational and social opportunities such as competitive games. A more complex, flexible pattern of withdrawal may be more satisfactory as it would allow for participation in all core subjects. This might involve use of a pattern in which children were withdrawn for different lessons each week, perhaps on a four-weekly rota. In particular, this could include occasional withdrawals from a subject the child is good at as he could easily make up the lost ground at school or through homework.

The role of the specialist teacher in both units and resource-room services would be to teach the child with visual impairments and also to enlist the support of the other teachers to ensure the child receives appropriate education in mainstream classes. Although integrated services for children with visual impairments are comparatively new, teachers of the hearing-impaired and remedial-service teachers have had a great deal of experience over many years in working with mainstream teachers. The 'tea money/ playground duty' approach, in which the specialist teacher makes a special point of volunteering for extra tasks which need doing, has been tried and tested on many occasions. But enlisting support requires more than this. A number of writers (Jamieson *et al.* 1977; Benton 1982; Millar 1986) have attempted to identify the information and skills needed by the mainstream teacher. The interested reader is strongly recommended to consult their articles which are based on giving the teacher a realistic expectation of the child with visual impairments. This is achieved by explaining the problem and limitations which stem from visual impairments, providing information on specific eye defects and demonstrating how specialist equipment and modifying teaching approaches can overcome these limitations. Their suggestions also emphasize the need for teachers to use appropriate teaching techniques. It may help if they are involved in decisions about the use of specialist equipment and materials such as white boards, large print or seating arrangements. School-based in-service training may help to create a positive ethos in the school amongst the staff. Of equal importance to the teacher will be the supply of specific information on the educational needs of an individual child. The specialist teacher will need to be seen as an accessible source of practical as well as material help, perhaps sometimes taking most of the teacher's class to allow her extra time with the child with a visual impairment. Enlisting the support and cooperation of the school staff will be critical to the successful integration and education of the children.

Peripatetic services to children in mainstream schools can also be divided broadly into two main types – the visiting-teacher services and the teacher consultant. Both types of services require the specialist teacher to be able to assess and teach children with visual impairments and to effect changes in the working practice of mainstream teachers. The extent to which they use these two skills will vary with each job. In practice, many teachers find they do both of these jobs and make a decision about which service to offer, based on the needs of a child at a particular stage in his education.

The visiting teacher will work directly with children either at home, as has been described with very young children, or at school. The work may well be in a specialist area such as mobility or braille, to follow up a difficult subject such as practical work in geography, or as part of an assessment over time, using specific assessment and teaching materials. Although the child will need the specialized skills of the teacher, there is a danger that these sessions are seen as meeting the special needs. The peripatetic teacher will need to ensure, from the outset, that the school and class teacher are quite clear about their primary responsibility for the child. The child must not be seen as receiving his education during the peripatetic teacher's visits and the teacher will need to work carefully in order to achieve this understanding. In the beginning, this will require a discussion between the peripatetic teacher and, usually, the head teacher and class teacher to negotiate the basis on which the visits will be made. This may involve an agreement on having the child withdrawn from the classroom and of enabling the peripatetic teacher to work in the child's classroom. It could well include having the class teacher available for discussion during the visit. It will need a contract, however informal, about the obligations of the two teachers on visits and provision of materials, record-keeping procedures and the content of teaching sessions. Without this negotiated basis for the visit, the special teaching sessions may not affect the rest of the child's education and may even hinder development, if there are conflicting priorities and approaches. Although, as has been stated, the peripatetic teaching service is found in a number of other countries which have staff: child ratios of 1: 8–1: 12, in England and Wales the service is more likely to consist of a specialist teacher advising classroom teachers on the management of a child with visual impairments. These advisers or consultants will have a number of roles and need a range of skills. Many of these skills are not specific to teachers of the children with visual impairments. The role of the adviser as advocate, the skills of organizing work time, of being an effective agent of change, for example, are all common to teachers in other areas of special education, to educational psychologists, social workers and many therapists.

Millar (1986) brought together information from a number of articles and research studies which identified what mainstream teachers wanted by means of support. Broadly, this covers 'knowledge of the problems of the visually handicapped' and 'practical as well as material support'. He lists twenty-five ways in which his service has attempted to provide this support. This list suggests the teacher should:

> Collate as much meaningful information about the child as possible.
> Assist in the development of personal organisational skills.
> With colleagues, plan teaching programmes and offer assistance with homework issues.
> Participate in curriculum development with reference to the special needs of particular visual conditions.
> Raise the level of teacher expectations in order to develop positive levels of achievement (p. 20).

Many of his other points are more specific examples of these general principles.

Taylor (1986) considers that among other aspects of their role consultants to classroom teachers should:

- explain effects of visual impairment;
- assess child's needs;
- advise teacher on planning programmes;
- advise on adjustment to teaching;
- assess visual functioning and develop residual vision;
- monitor visual condition;
- develop tactile and other sensory skills;
- help with self-organization;
- advise on resource material;
- provide in-service training.

From these, and other studies (e.g. Lomas 1986) emerge several elements of the work of the consultant:

1. *To serve as advocate of the child.* To ensure the child's needs are understood by parents and staff and that these needs are met.
2. *To ensure resources are available.* Usually, by assisting the school to obtain appropriate equipment or services.
3. *To train local personnel.* Through formal in-service training sessions and courses as well as less formal but regular sessions with individuals or very small groups of staff.
4. *To work as part of a team.* The role within that team will vary. It may involve liaising with other services and coordinating the work of other

professionals. It may involve acting as an important, but small, part of a team with a specific limited role. The skilled consultant would be able to identify his role clearly, usually by direct negotiation with the other involved people.

Dawkins (1990) described the design and administration of integrated services in a publication entitled *Bright Horizons*.

Factors Affecting Placement

At one time, blind children went to 'blind schools', partially sighted children went to schools for the partially sighted and the decision was based very largely on an assessment of vision by an ophthalmologist. Today, placement is usually based on consideration of a much larger number of factors which are known to affect placement, although some LEAs do seem to be moving towards an equally crude 'local school' policy. In an investigation into factors which affect success in mainstreaming children with visual impairments, Bishop (1986) identifies 69 possible factors of which 'amount of vision' was ranked 60th in importance.

What factors need to be considered when placing a child with visual impairments? How can we decide whether a special school or mainstream placement would be more appropriate? Some useful points can be found in small studies of anecdotal description such as that by Swann (1981). Other studies such as the one cited by Benton (1982) or Bishop (1986) make us aware of several groups of factors.

Firstly, there are those factors associated with the visual defect. The acuity itself need not be the factor which determines placement but the child's use of available vision, including speed of working and mobility, will indicate if he will be able to cope with the visual demands of a regular classroom. These demands will vary with different schools and subjects and the different ages. An assessment of functional vision (as described in a later chapter) will give the information necessary to make a judgement on the child's needs based on his use of vision.

The second group of factors can be termed social/emotional. There are several aspects to this. One is the child's personality – attitude to self and to others, competitiveness, motivation, sense of humour – what could be called robustness. It is an important element in the placement of any child but seems critical for many of these children. The child who does not have this robustness may feel under stress if placed in inappropriate settings and adopt stress reduction or avoidance strategies. They may move attention from the academic work through day dreaming, becoming aggressive or falling ill with unattributable pains. Children with failing vision will often lack this robustness and seem nearly always to get on best in special schools for a period of time.

A second element of the social/emotional area is social skills – assertive, conversational, non-verbal such as response latency, posture, direction of gaze. Nearly all research has shown that adolescents with visual impairments are below sighted children in these skills, yet many are teachable skills. Those children who do not or cannot learn them may have great difficulty in an integrating setting. There is support for the view that these factors are critical from Bishop's list of 69 factors affecting placement of children in integrated settings. The factors within the students which come clearly at the top of the list are: social skills, academic achievement (average or better), positive self-image, independent motivation (or 'inner drive'). The only factors ranked ahead of these are 'accepting/flexible classroom teacher' and 'peer acceptance/interaction'.

Another set of factors centre on the parents' attitudes and wishes. This is common to the placement of all children and not just those with visual impairments. Factors which may influence the parents' wishes for education may include the ease of communication and management of the child compared with some other groups and low incidence with thinly spread professional expertise in this area. The perception of need as very special, particularly with the totally blind, multi-handicapped or deaf-blind child, may also influence parents' wishes for placement.

A final set of factors are those concerned with the local provision of services and resources. While, ideally, it would be nice if placement were determined by factors such as those which have been described, in practice it is often the case that external factors such as the attitude of a head teacher, interest of an administrator or local financial circumstances, will be the ones that determine the placement of a handicapped child. Some of these factors are to do with services – the availability of a trained visiting teacher or peripatetic adviser, non-teaching assistants, units, special schools. Children with visual impairments may be few in number but have a heterogeneity of needs which call for a range of educational provision. The range of services is sometimes seen to be a hierarchy, from most desirable full integration to least desirable residential special school. This concept ignores the idea of appropriateness for meeting a child's needs but the same services seen as a continuum with open access between facilities does allow for the changing needs of children over time and the range of needs within the population. The existing provision, both in range and incidence, therefore will be a factor in determining placement options. The provision is likely to reflect the attitudes and philosophies of the LEA councillors, director and administrators and, in particular, their commitment to integration or to special education. Within schools, the attitude of the head teacher and the interest of all the staff will affect the services offered by the school and its suitability for individual children. For example, a special school with a teamwork approach involving parents, school-based staff and other support professionals may be ideal for a child with failing vision. A mainstream school with governors, head and staff committed to integration and welcoming support services could suit a totally blind child throughout his secondary education. But a special school with a narrow curriculum or a mainstream school with a head uninterested in children with special needs could be most unsatisfactory for a child with visual impairments.

These four groups of factors (visual status/social-emotional/parents' wishes/local services) will all influence the decision on which school should be chosen for a child. The child's educational need for equipment, resources and teaching support will be central to the decision and these will be examined in more detail in subsequent chapters.

Multi-handicapped Children

The majority of children who have visual with other handicaps receive their education in schools for children with severe learning difficulties (SLD). Teachers in these schools will often work with groups of children amongst whom there are many combinations of handicaps and they should be used to receiving and using advice from other professionals such as therapists and visiting teachers. Advice on special needs created by the child's visual difficulties will come from the peripatetic teacher/adviser if the LEA employs one. While this service often results in much useful collaboration and support, it is only fair to the teachers to point out that many peripatetic teachers of the visually impaired have not had teaching experience with this kind of child. Very few services are yet organized with specialized caseloads of, say, secondary, pre-school or multi-handicapped each allocated to teachers with appropriate backgrounds. Those that have this system, from anecdotal evidence, seem to be happy with the arrangement. The RNIB employs a team of advisers who do have experience of children with additional difficulties and they will visit schools at the invitation of the LEAs. Sense, the National Association for Deaf-Blind, also has a team of advisers who work as a Family Advisory Service. Based on London, Birmingham and Newcastle they visit families of young deaf-blind children and schools to offer advice and support. They also arrange short residential assessment sessions at their centres. Some SLD schools are developing in-school expertise in understanding children with visual impairments and an increasing number of teachers from these schools are applying for specialist training as teachers of the visually impaired. More schools are organizing in-service training in this field for their staff. The result of these initiatives can be a dramatic development in the quality of service offered to the children with visual impairments.

Some children who have visual with other handicaps are taught in a special school for the visually handicapped. The majority of schools now make provision for some children with combinations of handicaps. Two schools, run by the RNIB, have a national intake and provide specialist education for multi-handicapped children. Rushton Hall, in Northamptonshire, takes children of primary age including those with profound multiple handicaps. Condover Hall, near Shrewsbury, has children between the ages of 11 and 21 with special units for those with additional physical handicaps and for the deaf-blind.

School provision has always been more comprehensive than post-school provision for continuing education or life-long care. The situation has improved during the 1980s. The RNIB report, *Out of Isolation*, (Best *et al.* 1987) highlighted the urgent need for support to be offered to the adult centres which were looking after clients with visual impairments simply in order to enable them to maintain the skills they had developed while at school. At present no specialist advisers are available, although some help may be obtained from mobility and rehabilitation workers employed by social-service departments, and from the Multi-handicapped Information Service of the RNIB. Further education colleges, such as Queen Alexandra in Birmingham and Heatherset in Reigate provide increasingly for children with multiple handicaps and run courses in living, social and survival skills as well as more academic courses. The deaf-blind population is comparatively well catered for, although there is still an inadequate number of places. Both Sense (at Market Deeping and at Edgbaston) and the Royal National Institute for the Deaf (at Poolemead) run centres for deaf-blind people who need continuing education after school. Their courses are of fixed length, though designed for individuals, and the centres expect to have a throughput of students, although all three centres see the long-term placement of their students as part of their concern, if not their responsibility.

Summary

Current services are based on a continuum of needs and provide integrated education for about 50 per cent of the population. The special schools for children with visual impairments are currently developing a new role within the continuum of provision, while the peripatetic services are restructuring into teams with both teaching and advisory roles. In the future, it is possible that placement of children will be more precise as research establishes the factors likely to determine the best ways of organizing and providing integrated education and the within-child variables which determine the most appropriate placement.

CHAPTER 4

The Environment for Learning

A visitor was looking round the nursery for blind children and was immediately struck by the quietness and seeming lack of activity. Were the children frightened of the teachers? Was the setting providing very little stimulation? Were the children more handicapped and lacking in initiative than she had expected? Fortunately, she commented on this to the teacher who was able to give her an explanation. No, the children were not being suppressed or under-stimulated, but, in order to understand their environment, they needed to be able to hear. When the visitor entered the room, they noticed and listened intently. Their classroom was geared to enable them to get information about what was going on, by providing a carefully controlled sound environment.

Duncan is partially sighted and entering an infants' school. The class teacher has met him and his parents and is looking forward to the challenge of helping him integrate. She knows she will receive some specific help from the visiting teacher for his reading and writing, but what should she do to help provide the best working environment for him? Should she place him by her desk or near a window? Should she modify the wall displays so that he can see them more easily? How can she help him find work materials?

The environment in which children work requires careful attention and there are three aspects that need special thought – the visual environment, the sound environment and the tactile environment.

The Visual Environment

The visual environment may not need much attention in small familiar areas such as the child's home. Here children may well be able to find their way about with ease and locate toys and household objects if they are where they are expected. It is more important in large bustling and visually demanding areas such as the classroom, school corridors and playground. Here the right visual environment can make a vast difference to the ease with which the children fit in and work at their best.

In order to provide the best visual environment for a partially sighted child both lighting and decor need to be considered. These two factors are closely interrelated as the colour of walls, floors and ceilings will greatly affect the amount of light arriving at a working surface.

Lighting

At the outset, it is important to point out that good lighting is not the same as bright lighting. Children with different eye defects and levels of vision will have different preferred lighting levels. Some children, notably those with cataracts, may see best in lighting levels which are slightly lower than normal, as this causes the iris to open and allows more of the lens to be used for vision. The relationship between eye conditions and lighting, though, is not completely straightforward and each child needs to be assessed to establish his preferred lighting conditions.

Lighting can be divided into two types, environmental and task. Environmental light is the overall illumination of an area. It needs to be sufficient to allow people to undertake usually undemanding visual tasks such as walking round an area. In specialist schools for the visually handicapped the level of environmental lighting is often slightly higher than normal, particularly in corridors and stairs which may present the children with more difficulty than their sighted peers. In integrated settings, it is usual to leave the lighting levels as they are, as major reorganization of the lighting is not usually practicable. Visual clarity can then be improved by altering the decor through the addition of coloured stripes on corridors or white edging on steps. The second type of lighting, task lighting, refers to the light needed for a specific task that is usually visually demanding, such as a pool of highly concentrated light on a reading book. Task lighting should be geared to the needs of all individual children and this is generally achieved by the use of desk lamps. Several lamps have been designed for visually handicapped and they have common features:

- flexible articulated mounting to allow easy positioning at the best distance from the task and the best position in relation to the user;
- clamp, stand and wall mounting for ease of movement around a classroom;
- straight-sided deep lamp mountings to eliminate glare from the bulb;

- double-skinned lamp mounting to keep mounting cool if a tungsten bulb is used;
- diffused lighting to avoid harsh shadows. This is achieved by using translucent diffusers, carefully designed reflectors or fluorescent tubes.

Currently all suitable lamps have a restriction in that they need to be plugged into an electric socket. This limits the number of places where they can be used. The additional hazard of the flex can be overcome through the use of brightly coloured flex and plugs which help in easy location. In working out the best position of a lamp to help a child, there are several aspects that can be considered.

Figure 4.1 Illumination in a classroom comes from general lighting (e.g. windows, overhead lights) and task lighting (e.g. desk lamps, spot lights).

Position of Lamp
Often the most convenient position is behind the left shoulder so that the light falls on to the working surface without shadows being formed by the right arm. If the child is working at a desk with a sloping surface, this may be particularly suitable. However, there are sometimes advantages in having the light in front of the child, particularly if the child is leaning over the work and so creating shadows with his body and head, or if there is glare from a shiny surface reflected into the child's face. The classroom will need to be fitted with extra sockets on the walls at desk height and perhaps in the floor, to allow the use of a lamp at the correct position.

Distance of Lamp
The amount of light falling on the working surface varies with the distance of the lamp from the surface. If the distance is doubled, the light is halved. The most comfortable lighting level can be established by having the child attempt tasks of different visual complexity (easy reading, examining detail on a picture, writing) under different lighting conditions. The position of the lamp should be carefully controlled and the accuracy and speed of performance noted. It may well require several sessions for the child to become accustomed to different levels before an accurate judgement can be made.

Figure 4.2   It is important to position the task light carefully so that the child's head does not create a shadow and the light is not shining in the child's face.

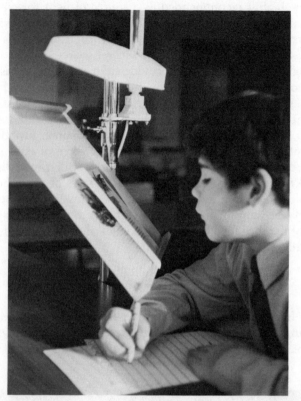

Figure 4.3   This shows good positioning with the light angled on to the page
and positioned to provide the right amount of light for the child.

Angle of Lamp
The lamp can cause glare if the mounting is tilted towards the child or if it
is positioned in front of and above the child. This glare will not only cause
the child discomfort but also prevent him from seeing clearly. The eye
will not be able to cope with such a high intensity of light at head height as
well as the comparatively low intensity at the working surface.

Environmental Lighting
There should be sufficient environmental light to prevent the creation of
hard shadow. If the level of task lighting is a little greater than the general
lighting level, soft shadows will be formed which cause little difficulty.

Having looked at the two types of lighting, we shall move to examine
the sources of light available to a child. The strongest and cheapest source
of light is the sun. However, it is notoriously unreliable and, although the
amount of light in a classroom can be partially controlled through blinds,

it cannot be highly recommended as a source of light for children with visual impairments. Suggestions on the position and size of windows are included in the DES Design Note 25, *Designing Classrooms for Pupils With A Visual Impairment* (1985). A second source of light is ordinary tungsten light bulbs. These may provide environmental or task lighting. The high concentration of light from a small bulb may give harsh shadows but these can be overcome through the use of an opaque shade. Bulbs become hot during use and this can be a problem when they are used in desk lights. Tungsten bulbs can be used with dimmer switches to give greater control of the lighting level. A third source of light is the fluorescent tube. This is cheap to run and provides widespread diffuse light. The tube keeps cool when in use and, if the ends of the tubes are adequately shielded, should be flicker free. It can be used in both environmental and task lighting and the most highly recommended task light for the visually handicapped contains two small tubes which can be turned on independently.

Decor

So far we have discussed lighting apart from its surroundings but the walls, ceiling and floor of a room will affect the amount of light arriving at a surface. Different colours will reflect different amounts of light, with

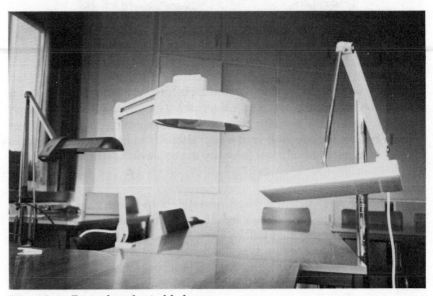

Figure 4.4 Examples of suitable lamps.

a glossy white reflecting some 80 per cent of the light falling on it, and a matt black surface reflecting almost no light. The texture of the surface – brick, emulsion paint, carpet – will also affect the amount of reflected light. The interested reader is referred to the detailed specifications included in the Code of Practice Handbook of the Illuminating Engineers' Society (IES 1977) and the recommendations given in the DES Design Note 25. The teacher needs to be aware of the position of the light source in relation to the walls, ceiling and floor in order to gain an impression of where the light the child needs is coming from.

A major problem with lighting is glare. This is much more of a problem than insufficient light. Glare can come directly from a light source or, as is often the case, can be reflected off a shiny surface. It can simply cause discomfort (as sometimes happens in large foodstores which have long aisles with a white flooring) or it can be disabling (as when dipped car headlights shine on to a driver's face). Of course, what may simply be discomfort to a fully sighted person may actually disable a person with impaired vision. Most glare can be eliminated through good design and attention to the decor.

- Windows should be kept clean or covered with blinds to avoid glare from sunlight as it is scattered through dirty glass.
- Shiny floors and work surfaces should be avoided. Both should be of low reflectance.
- Blackboards should have a matt surface. Where inadequate blackboards are already in a classroom, they can either be resurfaced or, in some cases, angled slightly downwards so that light from the ceiling is not reflected from the surface.

The interested reader is referred to the Code of Practice Handbook of the IES for further information on the design of lighting. This reference book contains details of all the variables which can affect the use of lighting as well as recommendations for lighting standards in the home and work places. Although the recommendations for schools indicates a level of around 400 lux (a lux is a standard measurement of the amount of light falling on a surface) in classrooms, the amount of light needed by children with various visual impairments will be different and so these recommendations can serve only as a starting point. Both higher than normal and lower levels will provide optimum lighting levels for individual children and a child's performance under different conditions needs to be observed to establish appropriate levels. Recommendations for designs are also found in the DES Design Note 25, referred to in the previous section.

In creating a good visual environment, there are further aspects of decor and design which need consideration. One key factor in visual clarity is *contrast*. Even without making any alterations to the lighting, improving contrast can help a child with visual impairment to make more sense of the surroundings. Look round a room or walk from the school entrance to a classroom and notice the visual ambiguities there are and the opportunities for improving visual clarity by increasing contrast. A silver handle merging into a white door; steps with no distinct edge to the tread; notices on coloured paper where the printing does not stand out against the paper nor the paper from the backing sheet; glass panels on doors which, although of wired glass, have no clear coloured stripe in them to indicate their position; doors of the same colour as their door-frames; white light switches on white walls; indistinct edges between the floor and the wall and between the wall and the ceiling. These are exam-ples you may well be able to find in your own situation. The decision about what action to take will be determined, not only by the need of the child with a specific visual defect, but also by the extent to which you want to provide a special 'easy' visual environment. Other people will have to live and work in the environment and so it may not be desirable, for example, to have a classroom which has large plain blocks of con-trasting colours on each of the walls. Well-presented and carefully posi-tioned displays will enhance the interest and learning opportunities for the children, but most of the changes which might help a visually handi-capped child will also be of direct help to other children by providing a pleasant but clearer visual environment.

The clarity of the environment may be particularly important for the child with severe learning difficulties who may not be able to move within his surroundings to check the information gained through his eyes. The child's 'threshold for confusion' from visual ambiguities may well be lowered because he is not able to incorporate context clues from previous experiences into his thinking. Although very little research has been carried out into the effect of the visual environment on a child's perfor-mance, it does seem reasonable to conclude that an unambiguous high-contrast setting will help the child. This can be achieved through the use of contrasting colours, patterned and plain areas and, for some children, a very small room, only a few feet square, so that they can see the limits of their surroundings and locate themselves within them. To this back-ground would need to be added items of interest to encourage children to look outside their own bodies for stimulation and information.

Sound Environment

All children with visual impairments, but particularly those who are totally blind, will need to use information from what they hear rather more than fully sighted children. If you spend just a few minutes listening to the sound in a classroom or at home, you will gain some idea of the kind of sound environment that the child is being offered. Is it meaningful? Will the child understand cause and effect? Is there variety and interest?

We need to examine two aspects of the sound environment – information and interest.

Information

The sound environment can provide information to help a child understand what is happening and to help in orientating to the surroundings.

Without effective vision to act as a focus of attention, the child has to concentrate on a person or activity mainly through listening. Imagine a totally blind child in a classroom. He may hear a door open and want to find out who has entered or left the room; he may hear someone near him start speaking but, because the speaker did not make clear who he was going to speak to, the child must attend carefully to try to work this out; he may be pouring some water into a glass and need to listen carefully to hear when the glass becomes full. These difficult tasks can be made easier if the relevant sounds – speech or sounds from the activity – stand out well from a 'plain' background. If a variety of sounds are reaching his ears, he will have to work hard to isolate the one which he must attend to and, inevitably, some of the others will appear more interesting! This skill of selectively attending and interpreting sounds is partly acquired through training but much can be achieved through creating a good sound environment.

Children can be helped through training to understand what happens when sounds are made. For example, they need the opportunity to open and close doors and have their attention drawn to the difference in the two sound sequences; they can be shown how to write on a blackboard with chalk so that they know what is happening when they hear the sound associated with that activity; they can guess which of two sounds is being made nearer to them and then walk across a room to see if the relative distances are as they expected. The environment can be designed so that there are no confusing background noises, such as a radio, which can mask useful sounds. If a working area can be separated with screens from a main class area, this may help some children by cutting down extraneous noises. Working in a corridor, while often quieter than a classroom, is not always helpful as the child may have to ignore many distracting and interesting sounds, such as staff and children erecting wall displays or moving equipment. A separate room off the main classroom is probably ideal.

A second type of information that can be obtained through listening is concerned with orientation. Again, this is likely to be of primary importance to the blind child but may also be of help to many children with severe visual impairments. Children can work out where they are within a room by listening to fixed sounds such as a fish tank or ticking clock; the sounds from a washroom or an office can help in judging position in a corridor; they can find their way across a playground by listening to a squeaky swing, a tree branch banging against a wall or a wind vane above a door. So sounds can help a child by indicating the direction and the distance of a feature. Some of the sounds that may be of help will occur naturally but others, like a cuckoo clock or wind-chime, can be introduced to make the sound environment more helpful for orientation.

Interest

As well as a source of information, the sound environment should also be interesting. Just as we create a pleasant visual environment to look at in our homes and work places, so the sound environment should be pleasant for people with visual impairments. Many classrooms have the variety necessary to gain and maintain a child's interest. An element that might need special consideration is a quiet area in which there is silence or at least the opportunity to think or converse without the presence of competing sounds. This is particularly important for braille users in a mainstream secondary school. They may make notes on a tape-recorder or a brailler but in both cases, there needs to be a room/area in which this can be done without the feeling that other people may be disturbed.

These factors come together and take on particular importance when working with the child with severe learning difficulties. Such children may have a minimal interest in their surroundings and, if these are confusing or uninteresting, may well look inward for stimulation. Spend some time just listening to the sound environment and try to identify

- what might bring pleasure or interest to the child;
- which sounds will help a child understand what is happening;
- what is in the surroundings;
- the position of the child in the room.

In trying to create an appropriate environment, start by looking at the size of the areas. Large echoey areas are difficult to understand as there is no clear indication of direction nor distance. A small area, just a few feet square, is much more manageable. Echoes will be reduced by curtaining and carpets and these can be used to advantage. Cupboards and screens can form sound walls to give an area a 'small' atmosphere. Different types of sound areas can be included in a room by the planned use of furniture and flooring and, inevitably, there will be different kinds of rooms within a school building.

The next stage is the identification of key sounds within the room. These will help in establishing fixed points such as the door, a wall, windows. Consider sounds from outside (a corridor, road) as well as those occurring naturally within the area. It may be helpful to introduce a few sounds such as a ticking clock over the door; a beaded curtain at the entrance to a storeroom; a glass wind-chime near the window. Interest can be created by variety and one way of ensuring this is to have blocks of time during the day in which there are sound-making toys that the children can use, tape-recorders, sound mobiles, conversation and silence.

The immediate working area around the child has received considerable attention recently and a number of centres are now using wooden resonance boards, based on a Danish design, in their work with severely handicapped children. These boards, often about 6 feet by 4 feet, consist of a plywood sheet raised off the ground by a one-inch-square edging round the sheet. The child lying on the sheet receives a sound 'answer' to movements of the limbs, and as the child touches, grasps or drops equipment. The vibrations and echoes are both useful and a board allows more freedom of movement than would a carpet or mattress.

Outside the classroom, corridors often have hard flooring and can be echoey but this may not be a disadvantage. The sound, or answer, children receive from their footsteps may be of considerable help compared to the deadened sound of a footstep on carpet. There will be some naturally occurring sounds off a corridor and these may be of some help to a blind child, but it is likely that the next area examined, the tactile environment, will provide more useful information.

Tactile Environment

In examining the significant elements of a tactile environment, we shall first discuss the close working environment and then show the need for an environment to help with mobility.

The working area for a blind child should be free of distractions as it should be for sighted children. These may be books and pieces of equipment left on the desk-top or small parts of the furniture which are tempting to fiddle with. The work area may be better for a blind child if there is a clear edge to it. Equipment can be placed on a tray or a rim can be added to the desk surface. Not only can the edge be used as a reference point for working out the position of an object, but it will also ensure the materials do not fall or get knocked off the table. It is often helpful if the child is allowed to explore what is on the working surface before commencing work. If necessary, a child's hands can be guided across and around the surface. This will ensure he is aware of what is in the area in front of him, something which might not happen if he is not directed to explore it. As the child tries to build up a clear mental map of what is in front of him, it can be helpful to ensure pieces of equipment are replaced in exactly the same place as they were taken from. This might be particularly important for a very young or mentally handicapped child who is being taught concepts such as 'in front of', 'at the side of', 'near to' and so on. In short, try to imagine the surface from a tactile point of view rather than a visual one. The main difference, as was outlined in Chapter 1, is that the hands cannot give information to the brain about relationships between objects as easily as the eyes. Children will need to explore an area systematically to feel and refeel the objects – to work out where each is in relation to the edge of the table and to each other. Generally this is easiest if the distances and objects are small – no bigger than a hand span. They will also need to identify the critical features of an object – whether it is a piece of educational equipment, a toy, a piece of furniture or a person – features which will enable the child to recognize the object.

A second aspect of the tactile environment relates to the wider surroundings used for mobility and orientation. This includes consideration of the layout of rooms, corridors and open spaces such as playgrounds. For many people with visual impairments there is a significant distinction to be made between familiar and unfamiliar surroundings. The former, such as a classroom or bedroom, may be well understood simply through having been walked round and used. A child may be able to orientate himself without being able to say how he knows where he is. In less familiar surroundings though, and for children who have more difficulty in learning, what are the clues in the tactile environment that may help in orientation and mobility?

As a blind child launches forward into a room, his perception of the room does not stem from his eyes at head level but rather from his feet. His interest is likely to be centred on the ground under the next step he takes and, unlike the sighted child, his 'view' of the room will be partly based on floor surfaces. So foot 'clues' are an important aspect of the environment. The other important aspect is information available to his hands. He is likely to use his hands to identify objects, receive warning of hazards he is approaching and to check where he is. Much of the information available from the tactile environment to both hands and feet will be from naturally occurring features, but some special clues can be added for a child having particular difficulties. Imagine a route from a school entrance to a classroom to give an idea of those elements of the tactile environment which need attention. Just inside the entrance may be a mat recessed into the floor but with a metal edge sticking up round it. Following the left-hand side of the corridor, there may be a trough with plants, a fish-tank (with noisy pump), a cardboard-box man made by one of the classes, a radiator and then the classroom door. The other wall may have a fire-extinguisher at head height and then, outside the secretary's office, there may be occasionally parcels of books, papers or equipment on the floor. Some of these features – the fish-tank and radiator – might give useful information to a child. Others – the fire extinguisher and boxes – are likely to be much more problematical and probably need to be moved. But the information in the corridor is probably sufficient to allow most children to cope with travel along it. Particular hazards such as half-open doors or steps may need special attention. Half-open doors should be avoided and warning of stairs may be given, if necessary, by the addition of a mat or texture strip on the wall. If the banister extends beyond the top and bottom of the stairs, then it is probably not necessary to provide additional information.

Open spaces are usually more difficult to understand and to travel through than areas such as corridors and small rooms which have continuous hand and foot information. The air space may contain sounds, temperature or smell information but will have no hand or foot clues. Foot clues may be added by using rubber mats or carpets if a child needs extra information but often the difficulty will be tackled by training programmes to develop mobility skills.

Assessment of Needs

Having laid out some of the elements in an environment that might affect a child, we shall now turn to the process of assessing the needs of a child for a particular type of environment. The 'ideal place' environment may be the easiest for a child but, of course, it may not be practical to create it. Particularly in a mainstream school where a child is using several classrooms, alterations to lighting, furniture arrangement or choice of classroom location may not be possible. The purpose of the assessment is to enable the teacher to make the best possible match between the assessed needs and provision. This match may include deliberately presenting the child with a challenge as part of his training. For example, the teacher might remove the extra support provided by a rubber mat which indicated the approach to a classroom, and so help the child to learn to estimate the distance of the door from the end of the corridor. For all children the sound environment will need to be considered and then the visual environment will be relevant to partially sighted children and the tactile environment to blind children. Some children with poor vision will also use touch for information and so they also should have their needs for a tactile environment assessed.

The assessment of the sound environment will be carried out by observing the child's performance under different conditions. Note how the child responds to spoken instruction in a quiet area and a classroom; estimate his ability to listen by giving him some activities which involve listening to speech – instructions and information of increasing complexity – against background noises; observe the child working on his own in the two situations and note whether he spends significantly more time on tasks in one situation. A child who has particular difficulty in concentrating will need a quiet distraction-free environment, as will a child who has a hearing difficulty or has not developed good listening skills. The child with severe learning difficulties may gain stimulation from a varied, interesting sound environment. Note the elements in the sound environment during a day and then decide if more interest, meaning and variety could be introduced. A record can be made of the child's subsequent behaviour to see if there is any apparent reaction through movement, concentration, direction of eye gaze or other signs of listening.

Assessing the visual environment is more complex. A number of observation checklists have been published (e.g. Langley 1981; Barraga and Morris 1989) which give a guide to the observations which need to be made. The procedure should start with a listing of the areas in which the child will be, e.g. corridors, classroom, stairs, toilet, gym, hall, playground. For each of these list the activities that the child will carry out, noting if they are near or distant tasks. Next it is necessary to establish how the child functions at each of these activities. This may require observation of the child carrying out the activity as suggested earlier in this chapter, or asking the teacher or child. Remember that lighting levels may vary at different times of the day and at different seasons of the year. In addition, some children may have specific difficulties, for example taking medication or when moving indoors from bright sunlight. Particular attention should be given to the child's close working environment, usually a desk top, to establish the best visual conditions for the range of activities the child will be engaged in. The teacher then needs to examine the areas that might cause some difficulty to see if any changes are advisable. These changes might be in *lighting levels*, perhaps by adding lights in a complex busy area such as a wide staircase or by reducing the amount of sunlight to avoid glare from large windows; they may be with *decor*, perhaps by adding contrasting stripes on the edge of steps or resurfacing blackboards to give clear script; they may be in *reorganizing* the child's or class teachers' routine, perhaps by seating the child in a different part of the classroom further away from the window, allowing him to leave class early so that he can travel, with his equipment, to the next classroom more slowly and safely or providing a darker photocopy of class hand-outs.

Assessing the tactile environment involves the same procedures as suggested for the visual environment. The child's activities can be divided into distance mobility – walking through a route – and near tasks – in this context, the ability to find equipment and books and organize it on a table top. After mobility routes have been listed, the clues available to a child and those actually used can be identified. The teacher can then judge whether extra clues are needed to overcome difficulties or training given for specific routes or the child's routine should be altered to avoid very difficult routes.

For near tasks, difficulties are very often overcome by appropriate organization of materials, and so during assessment attention should be given to how the child searches for equipment, where items are stored and the consistency of replacing books and furniture.

Summary

Many children can be helped by the provision of an appropriate environment, in particular when in fairly unfamiliar surroundings, although children with severe learning difficulties may need all aspects of their learning environment to be carefully arranged. The sound environment will need attention if it is to be interesting and also helpful in orientation. The visual environment, determined by the variables of light, decor and contrast, will be particularly important to those with residual vision. The tactile environment will be of significance to all blind children and to many children with low vision. The child exploring through hands and, for mobility, through feet, will need tactile clues from the environment and also surroundings which are consistent and systematically organized.

CHAPTER 5

Principles of Teaching

We have described ways in which a visual impairment can affect development and learning and examined the factors in the environment which need controlling to provide appropriate conditions for learning. Now we shall discuss approaches to teaching and do this by:

1. Identifying some general principles of teaching.
2. Defining special curriculum needs.
3. Describing approaches to teaching the special curriculum areas needed by children with visual impairments.

Susan Smith is the teacher of a class of infants in an urban school of 250 children. She has been told that Lucy, a 6-year-old girl, will be joining her class. Lucy wears glasses but still has very poor vision. She cannot read yet and colours in untidily using a thick crayon and jerky arm movements; she seems very quiet and unconfident. How should Susan change her teaching approach to meet Lucy's needs? What special equipment or activities would she need to provide?

Edward Stone is a peripatetic teacher for the visually impaired and has responsibility for Donna, an 11-year-old totally blind girl who is moving into a comprehensive school near her home. She received her primary schooling in a residential special school for the blind. What general suggestions can be given to the staff of the school? What additional teaching will he have to organize? What special equipment will be necessary?

Principles

It should be clear, from thinking about the difficulties that may be caused by blindness or a visual impairment, that simply providing a piece of equipment is unlikely to meet the special needs of the child. Providing a computer to produce reading material in braille will not help a blind child to read at the same speed as a sighted peer or help in understanding visual concepts that are read about, say, in science or geography. Enlarging print or giving a desk lamp to a child with partial sight will not teach that child how to scan through texts for key points, understand a diagram or graph which is only seen in part or help in using vision to walk confidently and safely through busy traffic areas. The child who has difficulties in learning will need special teaching, sometimes using technology to help him learn and understand. This special teaching can be achieved by the teachers adapting their teaching style and by giving attention to what is taught. The special teaching can be given either in a special school or in a mainstream class depending on the factors that have been discussed in the previous chapter on services.

There are a number of general factors that need to be considered when devising an appropriate teaching style for use with any child with a visual impairment and these can be summarized under six headings:

1. Position.
2. Presentation.
3. Experiences.
4. Expectations.
5. Giving information.
6. Speed of working.

The initial letters of these headings spell the word PEGS and, indeed, these can be seen as pegs on which to hang the various principles that are needed to cope with all aspects of a child's special needs.

Position

The child's work position needs to be considered. For near tasks, at a desk, too often a child develops a hunched posture. He should be able to work without strain on the back and neck. This will require attention to the chair and the desk heights to ensure he is able to place his feet on the floor and can bend over the desk without stretching. The surface of the desk could well be raised at an angle to allow work to be brought nearer to the child rather than have him bend over to get close enough to see clearly. Portable desk stands can be a convenient alternative to a special desk. If a sloping surface is used, there will need to be some way of holding books and paper on the surface. This may be through a deep lip on the lower edge or an adjustable bar, magnetized strip or large clip which would allow the material to be moved on the surface so that the relevant portion can be seen easily.

The work surface may need to be larger than usual to give sufficient space to arrange large print material and equipment. This will certainly be necessary for a child who uses braille. Braille writing equipment, braille books, tactile diagrams all tend to be larger than print material, and the child will also need space to arrange these items so they can be quickly located on the surface and not get muddled up. The child with partial sight may need to read and write at different distances from the work surface and so needs both flat and sloping surfaces on a desk. A chair on castors may help some older children move to a more comfortable position directly in front of the work.

If children lack access to a full programme of physical-education activities and are also unable to monitor their activities in relation to other children clearly, then they will have difficulties with posture which can affect their comfort while working, health and appearance. Attention to the ergonomics of the work situation is not a frivolous detail. It is basic to efficient working.

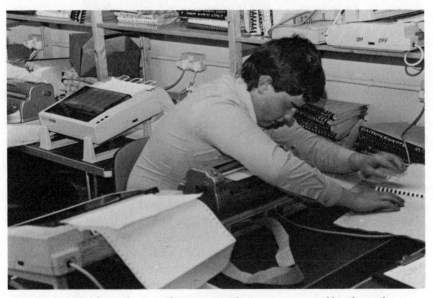

Figure 5.1 Children often need extra space for equipment and books and they need to learn how to use this space efficiently.
Photo: B. Dallimore, RNIB New College, Worcester.

Fig 5.2 (a) and (b) Use of a sloping desk stand can help provide a good and comfortable working position.

The position of a child in the classroom needs to be considered in relation to three variables. Firstly, there may need to be access to electric
sockets in order to use a desk lamp, a tape recorder, closed-circuit television or other equipment. This usually dictates a position for the child's
desk near a wall, as overhead and floor-mounted sockets are often less
safe and convenient. Secondly, the child will need an appropriate level of
glare-free lighting on the work surface. The level of lighting will be determined by the child's preference but is quite likely to result in natural light
from a window coming from behind the child, task lighting (if needed)
positioned so that it cannot shine directly into a child's eyes, and reflective
light from walls and desk tops reduced to a minimum through the use of
matt finishes. As glare is usually more of a problem than too little illumination, a position away from a window where controllable artificial light
can be used is often a good position for many children. Thirdly, there

Figure 5.2 (b)

needs to be access to stored equipment. Walking through a visually untidy and confusing class area will be slow and difficult for some children and walking while carrying equipment will preclude the use of hands for guidance. It can therefore be helpful if a child with visual impairments has simple routes to travel between desk and equipment storage. A child will be helped by having the opportunity to explore the classroom areas in the absence of other children and to practise moving through routes with some guidance.

The child's position in relation to the blackboard writing and any demonstration work needs to be considered and this may require the child to be encouraged to move to the front of the classroom to see blackboard work or to move closer to the teacher to see a demonstration.

Totally blind children and many of those with partial sight will use listening as an important source of information. The sound environment therefore needs controlling and the child may be best helped in a position where he can hear the teacher very clearly and work with a minimum of distracting sounds.

For multi-handicapped children, positioning will be critical when the child is unable to move around and so to find a position from which the classroom is visually clear and interesting.

Presentation

Visual difficulties can particularly affect access to print and the way this material is presented greatly influences the ease, accuracy and speed of working for a child. What elements of print need to be considered? Written material should be typed rather than hand-written wherever possible. Not only will this help by providing consistent letter shapes but the child who can see only a few letters at a time will be helped by consistent letter size and the straight lines of print. The contrast of the print and of pictures and diagrams, with the background is often critical. Blue duplicating ink and pink paper, for example, may give such poor contrast that some children with visual impairments would be unable to make out the letters. Letters which are overprinted on a background picture are usually particularly difficult to see. Black lettering on white paper is probably the best combination for most children, although there is some evidence that glare from too much white space between the letters and lines can create difficulty for some children. At least one publisher of large print books now uses a cream paper to avoid this problem. A number of children using closed-circuit television (CCTV) choose to use the reverse image mode and read white letters on a black background.

The size of print is most flexibly controlled through the use of individual magnifying lenses (low-vision aids (LVA)) or CCTV. These allow the child to read print of different sizes and require no special preparation of the text. Children usually need careful training to use these aids efficiently. Enlarging photocopiers produce text in which the size of print can be controlled and some children seem to prefer this mode and work more quickly with it. However, the same degree of magnification will not be ideal for all children and it must be remembered that some children, particularly those with a narrow field of vision, are actually hindered if given enlarged text on which they can see fewer letters at a glance.

The best size of print is usually the one which the child can read most quickly and accurately. The 'easiest' print may be larger than the 'best' print and the child may need several days' practice at a smaller print size before being comfortable with it and appreciating its advantages. The child will need to read as quickly as possible to succeed in education and so these factors surrounding the selection of print are critical.

Pictures and diagrams are usually easy to understand if they have a small amount of information on them. Very small print and print over a coloured background will add difficulties. Some children will find that small diagrams, perhaps covering no more than one-sixth of a sheet of A4 paper will be easier to understand than larger areas on which only a small part of the picture can be seen at one time. As with print, the contrast of the lines of the diagram with the background paper will be important. Bold black lines on white paper are often preferred.

The variables of size and clarity apply also to blackboard work, demonstrations and wall displays. Blackboard work will probably be seen only if the blackboard itself has a clean matt black or green surface. Writing should be in contrasting white or yellow and should have thick clear lines. It is usually helpful if the letters are carefully formed, of uniform size and arranged neatly on the board, particularly the beginning of lines which should start below each other. This will help the child find the text and beginning of lines – a skill which will be slow and difficult for many children who have reduced fields of clear vision. All displays should be prepared using similar guidelines and the finished product positioned at eye-height where it can be examined at a few inches away if necessary. White boards usually give very good contrast and can be useful if the child is not dazzled by the glare from the board.

It should be remembered that presentation of information in a written form can be supplemented with spoken information. This will be a quicker way of getting information for some children and through the use of tape-recorders can be provided fairly simply. In other cases, it will be necessary for teachers to add verbal explanations and descriptions of what they are writing or doing in order to enable a child with visual impairments to follow a lesson.

The presentation of material in tactile form to a totally blind child needs special consideration and is dealt with separately. The critical role of spoken information for these children makes the comments in the later section 'Giving Information' particularly important when working with totally blind children.

An additional element to be considered when working with multi-handicapped children is the definition of the working area. For close work there should be a clear visual or physical edge to the work area so the child can understand the limits of the area that needs attention and so some structure is put to the surroundings. The edge may be achieved by a tray or putting a wooden lip around the edge of a table. It may be helpful to work on a surface which is of a strongly contrasting colour to the surroundings. In both cases the child will need to be able to find out what is in the work area by tactile or visual exploration, usually with the teacher guiding the child's hands or drawing attention to the significant elements in the work area.

Experience

Children with visual impairments need access to first-hand experiences wherever possible. They should not have to rely solely on descriptions given by other people of situations they cannot see clearly. Those descriptions will not be as full or meaningful as a first-hand experience, will place additional demands on the child's memory, will appear to reduce the worth of the child's own perceptions and experiences and may remove some of the active involvement in learning through discovering. Even a simple action like pouring liquid from a jug is a much fuller experience when seen, compared to a spoken description of what is happening, and the level of understanding is likely to be much greater.

Children with visual impairments will almost certainly have reduced access to experiences that other children have – animals moving, looking into shop windows, seeing distant objects – and the lack of incidental learning has already been discussed. Some experiences, of course, will not be accessible to the children because of safety factors, cost or the limitations of their visual defect. It may never be possible, for example, for some children to see a valley or clouds in real life as their vision prevents clear seeing at the distances involved. (They may, however, be helped to understand the phenomena through the use of video tape or models.) Other experiences will be accessible if the necessary arrangements can be made. This may involve visiting places and making sure the child can peer at and feel the objects on display. Extra visits will enable the child to have experience of situations which may be commonplace for other children. For example, travelling on a bus for a young child with visual impairments may be an experience centred on an adult getting the ticket and then being hurried along to the nearest seat. Sighted children will be able to compare their experience with what could be seen happening to other passengers and could also take in other elements of the experience – people struggling with bags, the work of the driver, old people having difficulty moving on the bus, body movement of people on the seats, views from the window. To gain some of these experiences, the child would need to walk around the bus both when it is stationary and when it is moving, have time to explore features that are pointed out and be able to ask questions.

Expectations

It is often difficult to be certain what to expect from a child with visual impairment and to identify whether problems with behaviour, tidiness, application, concentration or neatness and so on are due to the impairment or to the child not making sufficient effort. In general, it is probably wise to require the same standard of behaviour from a child with visual impairments as expected from other children in the class, while accepting that the child's speed of working will be slower.

It can be hard work and tiring to be visually handicapped. A great deal of concentration is required for many activities – reading braille one character at a time; using a magnifying lens to study a section of a graph or diagram at a time; learning through listening without being able to watch the speaker's face – activities such as these require considerably more concentration than reading or listening with perfect vision. So it would not be surprising if a child had a lapse of concentration and missed a vital point or became frustrated when trying to understand a complex piece of work. This may be particularly the case for the child losing his vision or who has recently become visually impaired. The child may be best helped though if the same standard of behaviour is expected (although the degree of application may be greater) as this should help him fit in as a full member of the class. In a special school, it will be especially important for a class teacher to monitor constantly what is expected of the children to ensure that the very highest standards are being achieved. In this situation, it is easy to slip into an undemanding and over-protective routine. These expectations can apply to many small incidents in a day which can be significant in ensuring that children are working at their best. Examples are the speed of settling down to work, avoiding asking unnecessary questions of the teacher, fetching their own materials and equipment, waiting quietly. It may be particularly helpful to insist that children look after their possessions very carefully and have a system for storing equipment so that time is not spent trying to find mislaid books or equipment.

The neatness of written work, though, may be affected by a visual impairment. It is necessary to be aware of the inevitable limitations imposed by a particular type of visual defect and to take this into account in judging the effort that has been made by a child and the standard that can be expected.

Speed of working will almost certainly be affected by any visual impairment and this is discussed in a later section. Although the highest standards of work should be expected from a child with visual impairments, it has to be in the context of the reality that speed of working will almost certainly be reduced.

Giving Information

This section is concerned with teaching style and, in particular, the use of voice. To many children with visual impairments, a teacher's voice will be their major source of information. It is helpful if it is pleasant and interesting to listen to and it needs to give accurate information.

What elements make for a pleasant voice? The tone and pitch should be relaxed. Whether a man or a woman's voice, a relaxed tone is much easier to listen to than a strained or tense voice. You can hear a smile. The pitch and tone of voice can also communicate certainty, anxiety, boredom. These signals can be picked up by all children but particularly those who are not receiving the non-verbal clues such as facial expressions and gesture. Variety is important in making the voice interesting and pleasant. Speed of talking, volume, pitch, emphasis can all be used to give variety and make the voice more interesting for all children. It is invariably helpful for teachers to tape-record a lesson in order to study the use of voice and to identify strengths and weaknesses in their presentation of verbal information.

The accuracy of information is also critical. 'Stick this little thing through here and just look what happens – it all sticks together!' A sentence such as that is not unreasonable to hear from a teacher in a classroom. But it contains many inadequacies that could be improved upon to help a child not able to see the demonstration or process clearly. 'Stick' could be replaced by a more accurate verb such as 'slide' or 'push'; 'thing' replaced by the appropriate noun such as 'magnet', 'gudgeon pin', 'cocktail stick'; 'here' elaborated to the precise location. 'Look' might be retained. Visual words need not be replaced on the grounds that non-visual children might be sensitive to them. If the children are being asked to deduce and reach a conclusion based on a visual observation, they must be in a position where they can see clearly enough to do this or it must be recognized that the activity denies them access to that part of the educational experience. If an alternative mode of experiences is possible, for example, through touch, that opportunity should be available. In this situation, it is possible that touch might be practical, but not if it is likely to be that all the components no longer stick together! What may be important for all children is that they are given a description of exactly what happens from the teacher or another child. This rule applies also to incidental events such as a door banging, a window breaking, a child laughing. This needs to be remembered particularly if there is a change in the arrangement of furniture from, for example, the rearrangement of the classroom or the erection of a display in the corridor. The meaning of 'all' can be checked by most children through a quick visual glance. A child with visual impairments may have to rely on short-term memory only and so could be helped by a list of the component elements. The use of 'sticks' in the phrase with two different meanings should not cause confusion. Children with visual impairments should be able to cope with the same level of vocabulary and complexity of syntax as other children. The difference may come (as was discussed in Chapter 1) when words are used for objects and actions of which the child has no direct experience. For example, if the teacher were to add 'like bees swarming round a hive'.

The words will have to carry all the meaning that the teacher needs to convey as the additional information from body language (non-verbal clues) may not be accessible. Gestures pointing to objects, hand movements describing an effect, facial expression moderating a remark to make clear that it is a question or a joke – these ideally need to be replaced by clearer verbal expressions. It can also be helpful if the teacher develops a habit of alerting the child before information is given by calling the child's name and then speaking. This will enable the child to be clear who is being talked to and also gives the opportunity to 'tune' into the teacher.

The child is likely to have a clear idea of whether this kind of support is necessary and useful, although it may take some practice on the part of the child and the teacher to incorporate it into the daily routine. As a first step, though, the child should be asked if it is helpful and perhaps encouraged to discuss its usefulness after a trial period. Giving information with accuracy and using voice control may well result in all the children being offered better teaching!

Children with a mental handicap may need additional information. In particular, they may be helped by a careful guided exploration of the work area in front of them, usually the desk top. All the children with visual impairments will need to develop a technique for systematically gaining information about the work area, but these children may be heavily dependent on their teacher for guidance. The child will need to be made aware of the equipment that is in front of them and where it is located. Ideally, they should find out for themselves but, in being trained to do this, the hands can be taken slowly and systematically round the work surface. One hand can act as a reference point. It could stay in the centre of one edge with the other hand moving over the surface and back in different directions until the whole area has been scanned and the objects identified. Alternatively, the reference hand could be moved along one edge or side with the other hand moving across the surface and back to the reference hand. The extent to which touch on its own and touch with vision are needed will, of course, be strongly influenced by the level of vision of the child.

Speed

Speed of working has already been mentioned in the section on 'Expectations'. Here it is emphasized in relation to the time needed to undertake almost any activity. Children may take longer to find their place in a book, locate a piece of equipment, write a sentence, colour in a shape. They may need to peer, feel, check, replace, identify, absorb, put together and integrate as part of their exploration. Older students in higher education often find they have to spend many additional hours working in the evenings to get through their work at the expense of their social life. The non-visual child who uses touch will certainly need extra time to explore as well as to read and write. This applies not only to working at a desk. There needs to be time to explore a room and work out routes between areas; there needs to be time to integrate information coming through hearing when, for example, deciding where to sit in a dining room. Being rushed in work tasks or in mobility can be very frustrating or even frightening and this needs to be allowed for by the teacher.

It is unhelpful for the teacher to respond to this by placing the child with slow-learning children who, for very different reasons, may take a long time to complete work. It is equally unhelpful to use sarcasm or ridicule as a child cannot be embarrassed or chided into working more quickly than his defect allows. That approach will put additional stress on the child and may cause him to lose confidence and further reduce his speed of working. The effect of the speed of working can be most easily seen in an integrated setting, although most easily catered for in a special school. Perhaps it is inevitable that being visually handicapped will involve the child in some extra work time – a longer school day, school term or even school life – in order to get through the same amount of work as sighted children. Whereas in higher education individuals can be expected to organize their life in the balance between work and social activities, for a school child the staff need to make arrangements to allow access to a full curriculum through adequate teaching and study time to enable the child to learn.

Summary

Each of these six factors will affect the quality of education that is offered to a child with visual impairments, whatever the age of the child or the subject being taught. These are the background factors that need to be thought about and acted on in any educational situation. The summary lists below can be used to check that the major points have been considered. The action that needs to be taken will depend on the child and the situation in which he is learning, and the teacher may well want to provide a very non-specialized environment at some stage in the child's education to prepare for life after school. What is necessary is that all these factors are considered so that difficulties faced by a child because of visual impairment are controlled and the education designed to meet the child's needs.

A number of checklists are available which itemize the factors to consider (e.g. Jose 1983; Millar 1986; Chapman and Stone 1988) and many services for the visually impaired have developed their own lists. This summary is based on the factors identified above. It suggests factors that should be considered although, of the statements below, *not all will apply to every child.*

At the Desk

I have checked that the child's posture is comfortable for different types of work, e.g.

- reading;
- writing;
- craftwork.
- *Factors*
  Chair height enables the child to have feet on floor.
  Desk height enables the child to work with relaxed shoulders
  For braille reader, wrists and elbows comfortable when finger pads are on braille.
  Desk angle/height enables child to work with straight back, comfortable lower back angle, unstrained back neck muscles.
- *The work surface is appropriate*
  Desk-top size allows for tidy arrangement of materials and books.
  Desk top has rim to prevent materials falling off.
  Surface is glare-free.
  Storage in desk adequate for needed equipment.
- *Location of desk is appropriate*
  Distance for viewing blackboard and teacher demonstrations.
  Sound levels.
  Routes to door, storage areas, etc.
- *Appropriate lighting is available*
  Natural light from window is controlled.
  All light comes from behind or the side of the child.
  Task lamp, if needed, can be safely positioned to illuminate work surface.

- *Written material is legible*
  Letters clearly written or typed.
  Print and diagrams of good contrast with paper; size of print and pictorial material appropriate (with LVA or CCTV if used).
- *Braille reader is aware of material*
  He has had time to find out about whole of material.
  He has been guided through diagrammatic material.

Teaching

I have checked that:

- *My voice is*
  - clear;
  - audible;
  - varied;
  - pleasant.
- *My descriptions are*
  - accurate;
  - use appropriate vocabulary;
  - there when needed.
- *My preparations include*
  - high-quality duplicated material;
  - adaptations to diagrammatic material;
  - transfer of material to tape-recordings;
  - braille and tactile diagrams;
  - identification of potentially difficult concepts;
  - arrangements for seeing/feeling demonstrations and visual aids.

The Child

Does the child know *how* and *when* to:

- Adjust the work surface/desk for best use.
- Arrange material on the work surface.
- Plug in and position a lamp.
- Use a LVA efficiently (viewing techniques, care of aid).
- Use a CCTV (controls, platform, reading technique).
- Use a tape-recorder for listening and recording.
- Set up and use appropriate computer equipment.
- Explore tactile materials systematically.
- Ask for help.

CHAPTER 6

Access to the Curriculum

Simon is a 13-year-old boy whose hobby is looking after tropical fish. He is very interested in animals and seeks out nature programmes on television. At school he goes through periods of enthusiasm for science lessons if a topic is to do with living creatures. He is in all these respects an ordinary boy. He is also partially sighted and, although he looks after his fish with care, making good use of the vision he has, he does need help in using vision for mobility. At school he started to type as his handwriting is poor and this requires him to practise in the lunchtime when the typing teacher comes into school to give him extra tuition.

Simon is, therefore, a secondary-school-aged school child who, like other children, needs access to the full curriculum to satisfy his interests and to prepare for life after school. Because of his special needs (many of which were defined in Chapter 1) he also needs access to a special curriculum which will clearly include low-vision mobility and typing. This chapter examines ways of providing access to the curriculum. Special curriculum subjects are defined and discussed in later chapters.

Some curriculum areas can be made accessible through care in the presentation of material and through use of the principles of teaching described in the previous chapter. For many of the arts-based subjects – English, reading, history, religious education – this approach will go a long way to ensure that a child with a visual impairment can take a full part in lessons. Curriculum areas which involve practical activities create more of a challenge and will require adaptations in teaching approach and the support of specialized equipment. Science subjects, maths, art and craft and physical education are all likely to require this level of attention and particularly so if the child is totally blind. In all areas, though, the overriding concern will be to ensure the child understands the concepts involved in lessons. No item of equipment will do this. It requires the provision of expert teaching with, perhaps, support through the use of specialized equipment.

The introduction of the National Curriculum in the UK affects the education of children with visual impairments in three ways. First, the content of the curriculum requires children to acquire some skills and carry out activities which may be particularly difficult or even impractical, for example some of the activities in the mathematics curriculum which involve estimation. At the time of writing, groups of teachers are analysing all aspects of the curriculum as they are published to establish which aims will need to be modified and which could be achieved through the use of specialized teaching techniques or equipment. Their recommendations will form a series of guide-lines available through the RNIB. Second, the standards set in the Standard Assessment Tasks (SATs) and in General Certificate of Secondary Education (GCSE) may not be appropriate for children with visual impairments. The test items may need altering to be accessible to children with no vision. They may include diagrammatic material, for example, which will need to be transcribed into a form the children can understand. Items may need changing because of the great difficulties children may have in achieving the same level of academic and cognitive development, particularly in the primary years. As yet, no solution to this has been found although the National Curriculum Council (NCC) and School Examinations and Assessment Council (SEAC) are both sympathetic to the children's needs and are actively supporting the work of teachers investigating these problems. Third, the National Curriculum prescribes the subjects to which a great deal of teaching time should be allocated. Children with visual impairments need access to a number of additional curriculum areas (such as the areas discussed in Chapters 7–10). It seems most unlikely that these can be fitted into the school day and so will need to be taught after the school day or, perhaps, after the end of the school term. Again, the position will only become clear during the next two or three years.

While the introduction of the National Curriculum is resulting in changes in schooling, there are many aspects of teaching and learning which will remain unchanged by this development. The principles of teaching and the special educational needs remain and so it is possible to discuss these knowing they will continue to be relevant in the new situation.

Teaching Approaches

An adapted teaching approach may involve an increased use of verbal descriptions, explanations and instructions as was illustrated in Chapter 5. In a special class, the teacher is likely to spend more time talking with the children than if the children were non-handicapped. Although some of this time will be used in giving information, the use of questions is of tremendous importance. Questions may be used to check on a child's understanding of a point or concept, perhaps by accepting a simple restatement of the information or instructions that have been given, but more likely by questioning to elicit an answer which shows true understanding. A second type of question will require a deduction by the child through thinking about 'what if . . .' or 'how could. . .'. Another type of question encourages creative thinking and the use of imagination. Each type of question may be valuable for children who have limited experiences as they help them become actively involved in learning and give them an opportunity to get clear feedback on their ideas.

An appropriate teaching approach may use small-group teaching a great deal. This allows flexibility in the pace of the lesson and gives the child with visual impairment an opportunity to examine materials close to or to ask questions which clarify a confusing point. In some classrooms this help is provided by an assistant who works with the child or, more likely, with a small group of children, thus releasing the teacher to attend to teaching rather than to elaborating explanations. This approach may also be used as a central part of junior-class work. The special needs of the child can then be more easily accommodated by building on this existing good practice.

The organization of practical activities will require more detail than for non-handicapped children. This is not simply a question of needing more time to find, try out and record. It will be helpful if each element of the task is carefully identified and the children taken through the activities step by step. The children may need to be shown the correct way of completing a specific activity if they have not previously been able to learn by incidental looking. This can be implemented more easily in the special class, although it will be needed by children in other situations. The practical, rather than intellectual, elements of the task are likely to lead to tension. For example, in a primary maths project a child may be required to sort out a bowl of objects in different ways according to specific characteristics – colours, material, shape, use and so on – and to place them in different parts of a sorting tray. Identifying the object and locating the correct portion of the tray may take additional time, although the decision on where to place the object may be made as swiftly by all the children. Making a Mother's Day card is likely to involve colouring, cutting and pasting as well as decisions about what to put on the card and the wording of the greeting. The latter tasks may not cause undue difficulties but the practical elements may well need extra attention. If the card is to be folded, the child may need some help in aligning the edges using a template or a ruler. Before colouring, the desk will need to be tidy so that the area to be coloured can be seen clearly. In cutting, the child may be helped by a contrasting line drawn around the areas to be cut and may need help if this is not a skill used very often. The pasting should be carried out with each step carefully checked so that the paste is successfully applied only to the object to be stuck and the parts joined in the correct fashion. At each stage of the activity, the teacher's instructions will need to be precise and a careful watch kept on the sequence to ensure each step is correctly completed. This monitoring is something that other children may be able to do more of for themselves.

Equipment

Many items of specialized equipment are designed to give access to print for children with visual impairments. The main categories of equipment that convert information from one medium to another are outlined below.

Print—Enlarged Print (e.g. low-vision aids, optical aids, closed-circuit television, enlarging photocopiers, Viewscan, typewriters).
Print—Braille (e.g. computer transcription, Vincent Workstation, Kurzweil Reading Machine).
Print—Speech (e.g. tape-recorders, compressed-speech tape-recorders, Kurzweil Reading Machine).
Print—Tactile (e.g. Optacon).
Diagrams—Enlarged (see *Enlarged Print*).
Diagrams—Tactile (e.g. Thermoform, Minolta).
Braille—Print (e.g. Braille'n Print, Eureka, Vincent Workstation, Versabraille, Mountbatten Brailler).

In addition to these machines there are pieces of equipment that give support by making tasks easier. These include rulers with tactile markings, electronic weighing scales, speaking calculators and high-contrast marking pens. Each of these categories of equipment will now be described.

Print—Enlarged Print

The majority of children with visual impairments will be helped by enlarged print, although it must be remembered that a significant number will not. In this category, the LVA is the preferred equipment because of its portability and ease of use. Most LVAs consist of a lens in a plastic frame which has to be used at a specific distance from the material to be enlarged. The amount of magnification is fixed by the design of the lens. LVAs can be used with any print, although typed or printed material will be considerably easier to see than handwritten material. They may be

Figure 6.1   A selection of low-vision aids.

Figure 6.2   Most are used for printed materials.

Figure 6.3   LVAs can also be used for distance viewing.

used also with diagrams and with print on labels, index cards, notices, etc. Types of aids, their characteristics, and training for use, an essential element in ensuring efficient use, are discussed in Chapter 8 on residual vision.

CCTVs can be used for reading print and diagrams, although only a few machines have a colour monitor. Most systems consist of a camera mounted on a stand, a platform on which to put the material to be read and a screen which may be a television or a special TV monitor. Some systems allow for the camera to focus on material across a room, for example, on the blackboard, as well as printed material in books. The degree of enlargement can be controlled by the reader and so this provides a more flexible system, that copes with a wide range of print sizes, than an LVA. The degree of contrast and picture brightness can be adjusted to suit individual needs and the picture can usually be reversed to give a white image on black background, if needed. Recently developed systems have a split-screen facility to allow near and distant objects to be viewed together and to accept input directly from a computer as well as from

Figure 6.4 Closed-circuit televisions can help some children see print and diagrammatic material.

printed material. The degree of magnification is greater than with an LVA and so children with very low levels of vision may find a CCTV system particularly helpful. The disadvantages are cost and portability. Few systems are portable, although some can be transported between rooms fairly easily. In the secondary school, therefore, where they may be particularly useful in handling large amounts of print, a system is unlikely to be available in all the rooms used by a child and the child may need to withdraw to a central resource room to use the aid instead of taking a full part in class activities. Again, training for use can be critical and this, along with details of types and use, is discussed in Chapter 8.

Enlarging photocopiers have become increasingly popular during the 1980s and are now standard equipment in all special schools for the visually handicapped. Yet, in theory, their use should be very limited. They require each piece of material to be specially prepared and the degree of magnification should be adjusted for individual children. The

Figure 6.5   Closed-circuit televisions can also be used with typewriter and computer displays.
Photo: B. Dallimore, RNIB New College, Worcester.

resulting sheets, often of A3 size, are cumbersome to carry around and difficult to store neatly. The whole sheet is equally enlarged, although often some parts of the page or diagram can be seen more easily without additional magnification. Moving the head or paper about to see clearly is usually more tiring than using LVA or CCTV. The enlargements are not available for incidental reading such as labels, notices, and material outside school. The advantage may be in the ease of preparation for the teacher and the ease of use for the child (training is not essential). Although in the short term these may be persuasive advantages in an overcrowded school day, a child is likely to need another method of enlargement to cope with print after school.

The Viewscan machine is an electronic reading device in which the user moves a small camera across a line of print and the letters are displayed in a single line of print on an electronic screen. The picture is made up of small points of light and the size and contrast of the image can be adjusted. The system is truly portable, being no more than the size of a portable typewriter. The user needs to learn a technique for handling the camera. This is possible for secondary-age pupils, although scanning a page of print to find a phrase is difficult. The Viewscan cannot be used with diagrams. It costs about three to five times as much as a CCTV system.

Print—Braille

Several computer programs are available which enable Grade 2 braille to be produced from a standard keyboard (see Chapter 7 for information on Grade 1 and Grade 2 braille). They all require a braille printer, in addition to a microcomputer, to produce braille on paper and, costing at least £1,000, this is likely to be the most expensive part of the system. All the programs have some limitation. Most have difficulty dealing with maths notation and none can transcribe music. Although not all words will be correctly written in braille, particularly those that do not use contractions for syllables, the braille is usually very readable with only an occasional mistake on a page. Of course, the program cannot make decisions on layout and an experienced braillist will need to format and adapt text so that it can be read by a touch reader. The actual typing, though, does not require a knowledge of braille.

The Vincent Workstation is an example of a system which will transcribe print into braille, in this case through a BBC computer. The system also allows for speech or large print to be the output. A braille writing machine is included so that a child can type in braille and this input can then be converted into print or speech. The system has proved to be flexible and useful in the classroom for use by teachers and by children, although there are limitations on the amount of editing that can be carried out by the child. The equipment is generally mounted on a trolley which can be transported between classrooms which are on the same floor. The system was developed by Dr Tom Vincent to provide a fairly inexpensive way for blind students to prepare material for reading by sighted people. The addition of speech allows the student to review and check what has been written. Its use in preparing material in braille is an extra function which requires an additional braille printer.

The Kurzweil machine is a computer device which is designed for the semi-automatic transcription of print material. The print is scanned by a printer which recognizes the letter and can then output this as braille, through a braille printer, or as speech. The unique and sophisticated part of this machine is the camera which can recognize most common typefaces, though not handwriting. In practice, print material may need to be adapted before it can be transcribed to remove references to diagrams which are not reproduced or to add explanations for the blind child. Where this is the case, the material may need to be retyped. If a large amount of straight text is required, this can be a time-saving way of producing material in braille. The cost of the equipment is high, over £10,000, but developments, particularly in the camera technology, make it likely that similar Optical Character Recognition machines will be used very widely in the future.

Print—Speech

The particular advantage that speech has over print is speed of access. Most children with visual impairments read more slowly than a passage can be listened to on a tape-recorder. With headphones and a battery-powered tape-recorder a child has flexible access to print material. A compressed speech recorder will play back recordings at a higher speed than they were recorded at and so children can listen to material at a speed approaching that of silent reading – about 250 words a minute. Details of the use of these machines are given in Chapter 9 on listening. Tape-recordings may be particularly helpful for large amounts of text where speed and ease of listening make them preferable to written material. Shorter passages and instructions can be recorded and used by primary-aged children. Another advantage of tape-recording is the ease of making the recording. For simple passages, any adult or older child may be able to help. Care should be taken though with more complex secondary material as this needs to be read by someone familiar with the area of study, particularly if a graph, diagram or pictorial material is to be described. The main disadvantage of recordings is the difficulty of finding a particular passage and of studying lists of facts and tables. Pages of print are much more satisfactory for that type of activity. Details of the use of these machines and the preparation of material for recording are included in the chapter on listening skills.

Synthetic speech, as produced by the Kurzweil machine, may not sound as clear as recorded speech but with a little practice most listeners find it perfectly intelligible and acceptable. The speech output on Kurzweil machines is particularly good and uses an advanced system of emphasis, cadence and vowel sounds which take into account context and punctuation. Most computer output can be given in synthetic speech. The articulation will be clear enough to enable the listener to understand the output and ambiguous words or complex sections can be read out, a letter at a time, if necessary. This output will be a convenient way of monitoring what has been written and will be particularly helpful for checking the last few words after an interruption in typing.

Print—Tactile

The Optacon is the only machine which performs this conversion. It consists of a camera which is placed over print and converts the letter to a similarly shaped tactile image which can be felt by the finger. The display presents only one letter at a time and even experienced readers find they can only achieve speeds of 80–100 words a minute. The machine is more suitable for typed than handwritten material. It can be connected directly to a personal computer providing the reader with access to stored information. Many blind adults find the Optacon invaluable as an aid to checking print material where a large amount of reading is not required (e.g. letters, document titles). It is not generally used in the UK as a primary reading machine for children and is probably most appropriate as a complement to braille.

A training programme is essential for its efficient use and an excellent scheme for children has been devised by the manufacturers. This consists of exercises in the recognition of print letters, the use of controls which adjust the size of the tactile image, techniques of camera use, developing fluent reading through using syntactic and contextual clues. This may be given to primary-aged children as a series of regular lessons or, as it requires good motivation and application, it may be better given as an intensive block during secondary education when the child realizes its importance and will need to use the skill on a regular basis.

Diagrams

A high percentage of the information given to school children is conveyed through diagrammatic material and full access to the curriculum requires access to this material. Where the material is not large enough to be seen clearly, the LVA or CCTV may be of help, particularly if the child can see enough to gain a clear impression of the overall picture before examining sections of it for detail. Where a contrast in the picture is not sufficient for the child to see detail, then enlargement is unlikely to help and the material will have to be redrawn, or the child given a verbal description of it. Although in practice this latter solution is often adopted, it is clearly much more preferable to give children their own material to examine. In redrawing material, both size and detail need to be considered. The scale of the picture can be selected to enable the child to see as much as possible in one glance or a few eye movements. The details can be drawn to give high contrast between areas with clear lines defining objects and areas. It is often helpful to provide several diagrams, giving information to different scales, so that clarity of detail can be increased and the material made more meaningful. If the material is subsequently to be enlarged or used with a CCTV, then colour is likely to be lost and this must be borne in mind during the preparation.

Making tactile diagrams also requires careful thought so that the child, exploring with one finger, can discriminate between the different shapes and raised symbols that are used. This requires careful preparation of the material as well as good training of the children in the techniques of exploration. Most diagrams and braille are produced on plastic sheets through a process called vacuum forming. A master copy is prepared

Figure 6.6   Tactile diagrams. Examples of master sheets and copies produced by the vacuum-forming process.

Figure 6.7   A diagram produced using the Minolta stereo copier.

using card and textured materials or using aluminium foil. A special plastic sheet is placed over it in a vacuum-forming machine. The sheet is melted slightly and then sucked tightly over the master copy. When the sheet cools, it retains the shape of the master copy. Multiple copies can be made in this way. An alternative approach uses a special photocopy process developed by Minolta. The master is prepared using an ordinary pen on paper and this is then photocopied on to special paper and the black lines become raised. Details of these processes and their uses are included in Chapter 7 on Tactile Skills.

Braille—Print

The technology described above gives teachers the means of preparing material for children. Braille-reading children educated in an integrated situation, and blind adults in employment need to prepare texts which they can read but which can also be read by sighted teachers or colleagues. In the 1970s this was a major problem, but there are now several machines to enable them to do this. All have braille keyboards and contain a transcription program within them so that Grade 2 braille can be printed out in English text. Perhaps the most sophisticated of these machines is the Versabraille. This is a portable computer with full word-processing facilities, a built-in disk drive and 20-character braille display. The machine is powered by a rechargeable battery and so can be carried around by a child for use in any classroom. It is almost silent in operation and this can be a considerable advantage over a conventional mechanical braille writer. It is compatible with other microcomputers and can receive text which is then converted into Grade 2 braille or can unload files into other machines. The word-search facility, when it was introduced, was a revolutionary concept for braille users as finding a specific sentence or part of a text in conventional paper braille was a time-consuming and often frustrating process. The Mountbatten Brailler which has been developed in the UK is capable of many of these functions, given additional hardware and software, and this may possibly become the standard braille-writing machine in the future.

Other Equipment

Much standard classroom equipment can be used by children with visual impairment, particularly when it is strongly coloured and so easily seen, or where there is a sound produced by it. For example, click wheels for measuring distance can be used by children with visual impairments and by sighted children; timers having large bold figures, designed for small groups, will be useful to many children; plastic hoops for use in the gym are usually brightly coloured. The RNIB publishes a catalogue of equipment specially designed for use by people with visual handicaps. This includes several pages of items specifically for use in schools, such as measures, clocks, timers, thermometers, maps, compasses, balls, jigsaws and games. For secondary-aged blind children, there are a number of electronic devices with sound or speech outputs which will be relevant to science work. Computers with speech output can be used to help with many types of calculation.

Using the Technology

How can a special teaching approach and specialist equipment combine to give increased access to the curriculum?

A number of publications give specific suggestions on teaching, for example, in maths and science (Fletcher 1970; Heritage 1986; Chapman and Stone 1988; Clamp 1988), physical education (Woods 1979; Buell 1983; Fullwood 1984), English (Norris 1972; Scholl 1986). Here are two examples to illustrate the kind of process that may be involved.

In a secondary project on local history, the class is to collect the names of streets and districts to find out their derivation and identify any links with local history. In the class is Adam, a boy who has cataracts with nystagmus which, with glasses, allow him to see print only with a magnifying lens. He can see sufficiently to walk safely in familiar areas but is very underconfident in unfamiliar places.

The project starts with an examination of a current street map and will also use a large-scale Ordinance Survey map of 1901. The quality of printing in the index and maps is poor and enlargement would simply exaggerate the defects. Other pupils in the group therefore study the maps and Adam is assigned to record the names of streets using his typewriter. The names have then to be grouped in some way and Adam, familiar now with all the names, can contribute equally to this part of the exercise. To do this he will be relying on his memory as it will not be possible for him to scan quickly through the list as the other children do. A pattern emerges for some of the streets where the names refer to trees and to girls' names, but the main roads and some of the smaller through roads do not fit into this pattern. The group turns to the older map. This is a photocopy which, despite its age, is quite clear as there is little information on it. The teacher has provided Adam with his own copy of this (at its original size) which he can examine using his lens. He has been taught to scan over the map efficiently, identifying the main parts – scale, key, title – and locate the area with which they are concerned. The other children can relate the streets on the older map to the current pattern, although Adam, not having studied the street map, has to listen to the other children making their discoveries.

They have now identified those roads which pre-date 1900 and can list their names – Bristol Road, Selly Road, Serpentine Road, Edmund and Christopher Streets, Bournbrook Lane. An explanation of these names requires study of books covering local history and this is what they will do in the next lesson. Before this happens, Adam ideally needs to spend some extra time trying to gain access to the street map. A CCTV may help him to see part of a map at a time. As he is now familiar with the area, he can anticipate what the printing may mean. If he uses an LVA, he may well be helped by a photocopy of the map on which the main roads have been highlighted in one colour and some of the other roads and estates identified in other colours.

In the next lesson, the pupils start examining the source material, skimming through indexes, section headings, glancing at photographs, making notes. Adam is fully familiar with this process and well able to make decisions about the significance of some information, but he does work more slowly than the other children and contributes less to the information they collect. On occasions, the teacher prepares material for Adam on tape (she actually gets her mother-in-law, a retired teacher, to do it) but for these short passages Adam can find a relevant piece and read it more quickly than the time taken to listen through sections to get to the passage. The other pupils have agreed that it is fairer for Adam to have the opportunity to take this role, rather than simply to be the group 'secretary' for the whole project. The group find out that Edmund and Christopher were the sons of a land and factory owner in the mid-1800s who named streets of workers' houses after each of his children. They discover that Selly is an old English name for willow tree and guess that the park at the top of that road must have been planted with willow trees at some time. Serpentine Road appears to be very old and Adam is able to suggest that it probably got its name from its shape as it winds, erratically it appears, round the edge of the church ground and up to the park – the shape is very clear to an LVA user! It is also Adam who first thinks of Bristol Road being named through the direction it goes. This is confirmed by a small-scale map of the whole area on which the road, marked clearly as a main road, is shown running out of the city towards the South-west and Bristol. The project continues with a visit to the shopping centre, the library and a talk about parish boundaries with the vicar before a report is compiled.

Adam has been able to contribute very satisfactorily to the group work through a little careful preparation of material by the teacher, earlier training in study techniques and typing and the creation of an accepting and supportive attitude in the class. In the future, the use of interactive video may well give pupils like Adam easier access to pictorial, textual

Fig 6.8 (a), (b) and (c) Learning in an integrated setting. A partially sighted child joins in project work with a colleague.

Figure 6.8 (b)

Figure 6.8 (c)

and spoken information so that they can take a more equal part in the project work.

In a primary school, the class teacher is introducing the concept of estimating to a class of 9-year olds. The class includes Deborah, a girl with Albinism. She reads print and uses a CCTV recently purchased by the LEA. Very underconfident in class, she often asks questions of the teacher, leaving her place to come to the front of the classroom, and needs frequent encouragement to produce work on her own. The teacher starts by asking questions about guessing the number of children in the group, the number of pages in a book, the height of certain children. Children's replies are written on the blackboard as they are called out and then these answers discussed in relation to the correct answers. Deborah, sitting at the front of the class, has the opportunity to join in as the teacher moves near to her desk when she shows the class the book and selects the child next to Deborah when they guess height. At each stage the teacher remembers to review the material on the blackboard by reading out the answers that were given. (If she had developed her use of an LVA, Deborah might have been able to use it to see the blackboard, but at this stage needs to rely on the teacher for information.)

The children are then each given a worksheet and expected to estimate the size of objects without the use of rulers. Deborah moves her chair to

Figure 6.9 (a) and (b)   A totally blind child helps in a weighing experiment
and discusses the results.

the adjacent table where her CCTV is located, switches on the machine and reads her worksheet. The sheet has been typed for Deborah by the school secretary but it has been agreed that all the children can have a copy of any work prepared in this way. However, the teacher sets much of the work directly from the class maths workbook, as this is considerably easier than preparing worksheets which require diagrammatic material to be drawn by the teacher after the typing has been completed. Deborah fiddles with the CCTV controls to get a clear picture of the best size – after a series of half-hour sessions with a visiting teacher for the visually handicapped she will be able to do this in just a few seconds – and reads the first question out loud. It is to estimate how many desks would fit along one wall of the classroom if they were placed close to each other. Deborah, unnecessarily, pushes back her chair, switches off the machine and wanders down to the end of the classroom to start tackling the problem. The teacher promptly spots the time-wasting element of her behaviour and, having discussed the CCTV with the visiting teacher, calls Deborah back and has her switch on the machine again, leaving the worksheet under the camera. She does, though, recognize the need to move around the room to carry out the estimation and encourages her then to get on with the task.

When Deborah is ready to write down her first answer, she moves to her own desk, using a second sheet to write on. The teacher is expecting this to be only a temporary situation until Deborah can use the CCTV more confidently and take out and reposition worksheets without difficulty. The teacher keeps an eye on Deborah as she organizes herself. She knows that if Deborah keeps felt-tip pens in a box at the back of the desk and replaces each one after it is used, if her ruler is in front of the box and little else is on the desk, then there is a good chance she will succeed in writing without knocking anything on to the floor. Deborah bends right over work to write, but the teacher notes she no longer needs the cushion to raise herself to a more comfortable position for writing. Fortunately, Deborah seems able to see well enough without the CCTV. That is a complex skill to learn. Perhaps, in the future, when she has to spend more time writing, she will find a portable sloping desk stand helpful.

As Deborah works through the exercise, she comes across a question which involves estimating how many whole squares on a grid are taken up by a picture of a boy. Deborah moves the picture around on the CCTV, able to see only half the outline at a time. Her teacher sits down beside her and, looking at the picture, decides to outline the boy in a thick black felt pen. Now that the outline is clearer (although the black and white picture does not show up the contrast between drawing and grid very well – a dotted line for the grid or colour monitor would be better), she takes a piece of card and, covering most of the outline helps Deborah systematically to count the squares as she moves the card to uncover more of the outline. Later she will learn that a masking control on the CCTV will perform the same function as the card and that it can be helpful in keeping on the line in reading as well as for diagrams. We leave the classroom as the teacher is asked by Deborah if she can stand on the desk to see where the top of the CCTV is in order to estimate its height.

CHAPTER 7

Tactile Skills

In Chapter 1 we examined some of the special educational needs that can be created by blindness and visual impairment but have emphasized throughout that children with visual impairments are primarily children. They have a multitude of aspirations, interests and abilities which are only partly determined by their visual problems. Their educational needs are similar to those of other children. They need access to a full curriculum, although their sensory impairments will create some additional needs that will require an additional special curriculum. In previous chapters we examined how access to the regular curriculum might be achieved. What extra subjects may children need to be taught? What special skills may a child need to acquire?

The child who is totally blind will need to develop tactile skills and learn to read and write in braille. Children with partial sight may need help in developing their use of residual vision so they can function efficiently both in and out of the classroom. All children with visual impairments will need to develop listening skills for use in the classroom and in mobility so that they can concentrate on, and interpret, important sound information. Some children will need help in developing movement, mobility and orientation skills. Under this heading come some daily living and social skills – for example, dressing, cooking, using facial expressions. These may have to be learnt when lack of vision prevents them being acquired incidentally. These are the four main areas in which some special teaching may be needed and each of these topics will be considered in the following chapters.

Braille

In this chapter, we shall consider the skills needed in braille reading and examine ways in which these can be developed from the pre-reading stage through to the use of speed-reading techniques. We shall also consider the technology that can help in the reading and writing of braille. Following this, we shall examine the production and use of tactile diagrams and maps and, finally, explore ways in which touch and tactile experiences relate to the education of children with multi-handicaps.

Braille Code

The Braille Code consists of shapes made out of combinations of six dots. The dots are arranged in a cell consisting of two vertical rows of three dots. This cell is of a standard size. The shapes formed by these combinations represent each letter of the alphabet and punctuation signs and the code that results from these combinations is called Grade 1 braille.

Braille is much more cumbersome than print because each letter has to be large enough to be felt clearly by the reading finger. It is also much slower to read than print because the finger can feel only one shape, or letter, at a time. In order to overcome these problems, braille uses a further set of cells, or combinations of dots. These are used to represent common sequences of letters and frequently used words. Many of these shapes contain only some of the six dots and so there are over 150 possible combinations available. This more complex version of braille is called Grade 2 braille and it is this version which is the standard in publications and is most widely used by children.

Grade 2 braille has several ways of saving space and making reading, and writing, quicker. There are contractions, which are cells representing common combinations of letters such as con, ea, er, gh, ou, sh, th. There are whole word signs in which one sign represents a word such as b for 'but', l for 'like', q for 'quite'. Contraction signs can also be used as whole word signs, for example 'ou' on its own means 'out' and 'sh' on its own means 'shall'. Abbreviated words take on a short form by using just two or three letters such as in 'af' for 'after', 'll' for little, and 'tm' for tomorrow. Some of the signs have several different meanings depending on whether they occur at the beginning, in the middle or at the end of a word. For example, one sign is used for the contraction 'dis' at the beginning of a word; the same sign means 'dd' in the middle of a word and represents a full stop at the end of a word.

Braille, therefore, is a complex code and there is more to learn than when using print. For children, of course, it is acquired as a 'first language' and so they do not need to learn the rules. The code does, though, impose a heavy cognitive load on the learner and even some computer programs have difficulty with some of the more complicated rules. For example the sign for 'th', like most contractions, can be used only when it would not confuse the reader scanning along the word with one finger. The word 'carthorse' therefore does not use this contraction. This, and many other exceptions, need to be built into computer programs so that they can produce correct braille for the reader.

Braille Reading

In teaching children to learn braille, what skills are we aiming for? What skills do they need? They can be divided into two main areas. Firstly, reading in braille requires all the skills of reading – blending, memory, using syntax, sequencing and so on. It must be remembered that reading braille is essentially the process of reading – attaching meaning to symbols. The second area concerns the use of fingers and the way in which the brain can perceive the tactile shapes that represent letters. This second area involves training the fingers and hands to move efficiently over pages of braille and teaching the brain to make sense of the raised dots that make up the braille code.

Good braille reading technique is based on *a smooth, light, left-to-right movement of one finger*. Each element of the movement needs to be developed through pre-reading and early reading practice. This is a critical stage in education as the braille reader is unlikely to come across braille symbols incidentally and so arrives at school without the years of exposure to letters that the print reader has. The smooth movement is necessary to ensure speed in reading. It helps a continuous stream of information to be received rather than blocks of information. In this way, the reading process is different from print reading. In finger reading perception takes place only when the finger is moving over the braille, whereas the eye sees groups of letters when it is stationary on them. The smooth movement will also help the reader stay on the correct line. With a perceptual 'window' of only one cell (again, different from the eye which can see several letters or words at a time) the reader can easily stray off the line. With a smooth movement towards a finger of the second hand, acting as a marker near the end of the line, efficient reading is more likely to be achieved.

Light pressure is needed to feel the bumps clearly. Nerves in the finger are better able to pick up undulations in a surface if the friction between the skin and the surface is reduced. This phenomenon is well known to craftsmen in metal – whether in high-quality cars or creative work – who often wear thin cotton gloves when examining a surface to be better able to detect irregularities. The reason for this is that, as the finger moves across a bump, two forces act on it. One sheer force acts parallel to the surface of the paper and drags the finger across the surface. The second, normal force acts at right angles to the paper's surface as the finger presses down on it. It is this second force which is used to detect the braille dots. With the sheer force reduced through a light touch, the brain can receive undistorted information about the dots and their relative positions and so is able to gain the clearest image of the cell.

Left-to-right movement is necessary to develop accurate reading and a good speed of reading. Some readers, particularly those given inadequate pre-reading practice, develop the bad habit of 'scrubbing' the cells – moving the fingers up and down and back and forward over the cell. These movements slow down reading and can also cause inaccurate reading as the brain becomes confused about the orientation and relative position of the dots. A left-to-right movement also allows the reader to perceive the cell as a shape rather than analysing it as a series of dots. This seems to result in quicker identification of the cell's meaning. Researchers investigating the recognition of braille cells (e.g. Millar 1985) found this consistent with an explanation of the process of spatial coding (using the right hemisphere) which requires the perception of global shapes rather than the identification of a sequence of dots.

Good readers usually develop one dominant finger and this is often the first finger of the left hand. It is possible that the left hand is preferred as it is linked to the right hemisphere of the brain which specializes in encoding spatial information. This means that the information can be sent directly to the right hemisphere where it is efficiently analysed, and then the information transferred to the left hemisphere (which specializes in verbal information) where it is named. Although the evidence for this is not absolute a number of writers suggest that this is likely to be the case (Hermelin and O'Connor 1971; Loomis 1981; Young 1982). A second finger or second hand can also have a valuable part to play in reading, as we shall see later.

These then are the essential elements of a good finger movement. How can they be developed? The principle is that practice should involve exercises which, initially, have no reading component to them. Children should be taken through a sequence of exercises which start by using real 3-dimensional objects. From these, the children should be exposed to raised tactile forms on paper and plastic sheets. These will not be representations of objects (which are very difficult for a blind person to understand) but abstract shapes and textures which the children can sort, match and identify. After this '2-dimensional' work, the child will be introduced to braille dots, not initially as letters but as shapes and lines. Through these activities the brain will gradually be trained to identify the shapes which the fingers are feeling.

The sequence of objects to 'pictures' to letter shapes and then words is similar to the sequence used by children learning to read print. Even the terminology used for objects which are felt (3-D) and shapes on paper (2-D) is similar, although the '2-D' forms do have a third dimension, depth, which can be used as a variable in the exercises.

Very early tactile experiences will encourage a child to explore with each hand and then with both hands together, moving the hand from a typical position near the shoulders, to become a useful source of information. Direct work on pre-reading will start with exercises using objects. These can involve activities to develop finger movement and strength such as taking clothes pegs off the edge of a tin, threading activities, using sand, water and playdough. A second set of exercises introduces tactile sorting and matching, for example, using building blocks, sorting cutlery, paper and other materials. Use of touch can also be developed through tactile labels around the house or school, on clothes, doors, pegs, chairs and drawers. Children also need practice in making patterns and developing an awareness of left and right. This could be achieved, for example, by placing objects in egg boxes, patterns with peg boards, copying models in plasticine.

'2-D' work may be largely based on vacuum-formed material with shape, size, length and texture discrimination and matching. A left-to-right finger movement can also be developed at this stage. The use of braille dots will form the latter part of this stage with lines and cells to spot the odd one out, matching the sample at the beginning of a line, and finding two similar cells in a line. This practice with braille dots will also develop the smooth, light left-to-right movement. This is unlikely to be successful if the child has also to figure out the meaning of the cells and link these together to make words. There will even be the need for some hand-movement practice to be separate from the discrimination and matching activities that will be used at this stage. Many useful suggestions for games and activities at this developmental stage can be found in Mangold and Olson (1981). These will develop control of the fingers and independent movement and strength. Practice in the use of hands for gaining information should lead to accurate tracking of a line of braille.

Another set of factors needs to be considered to ensure the development of reading techniques and these involve elements in the environment for the reader and attention to the use of hands and fingers. These factors are summarized in the diagram.

We start with four factors that have been introduced in the previous section on finger movements.

Use of Pad
Braille is felt with the pad of the finger, the area between the tip and the first joint. The tip of the finger is not large enough, nor does it have appropriate nerve endings, to be used for reading. In young children, the pad is likely to

be only just large enough to feel a whole cell in one movement but by the age of 10 most children will be able to establish which part of their pad they feel most comfortable using.

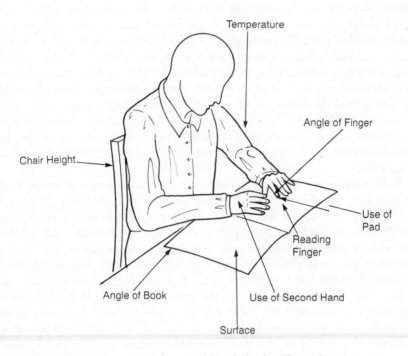

Figure 7.1   Critical factors in the use of hands for braille reading.

Angle of Finger
As the finger moves across a line of braille, the angle of that finger to the line will alter. It is likely to be at right angles, while the finger is in the middle of the line, but moves to a different angle towards the end. Beginning readers may be helped by ensuring that they maintain the same angle to the line as they move along it. This should result in consistent information being received about the orientation and shape of the braille cell. To achieve this, the child needs to make a movement from the wrist as the line is read.

Reading Finger
The choice of reading finger has been mentioned already in relation to the interpretation of tactile information by the brain. Although beginning

readers can be encouraged to read primarily with the first finger of their left hand, with experience, some children will choose to use a different finger. It is not reasonable to deny them the use of that finger if they have a clear preference for it. Experienced readers use different fingers although most good readers do use the first finger of their left hand. What seems to be important is that there is a primary reading finger, although, as we shall see, there is a role for a number of fingers during the reading process.

Use of Second Hand

In the reading process, the reader has to sweep along a line of cells. At the end of the line, the finger has to move to the beginning of the next line and then start to move along that line. This movement involves finding the next line and locating the beginning of that line. This complex activity can slow down the speed of reading and many good readers use both hands. This speeds up the process, particularly at the end of lines. For a reader primarily using a finger of the left hand, the right hand can take over reading the last few cells of a line, while the left hand simply moves down to the beginning of the next one. It is then ready to continue covering the text as soon as the end of the previous line has been reached. This 'scissors' movement is reversed if the reader has a dominant right hand for reading. Efficient use of both hands for reading will require practice and encouragement from the teacher. The technique may be best developed using pages which are not read but rather simply skimmed. Perhaps the teacher can tap out a rhythm to pace children until they become fluent in the technique.

Temperature

Cold fingers have reduced sensitivity and sweaty fingers stick to the braille paper. The temperature is therefore important in enabling braille readers to function efficiently. Reading may be difficult straight after coming in from a cold playground if gloves have not been worn. In summer, it is helpful to have talcum powder available to sprinkle on a finger if a child's hand is very hot. Incidentally, good readers will need to have clean fingers.

Chair Height

Some experienced braille readers prefer reading with a book on their knees. Finger reading requires the hands and forearms to be able to move easily over the book surface and for some readers, this is easier if the book is placed in a lower position than would be comfortable for reading print. The wrists and shoulders should be relaxed, if reading is not to be tiring, and so some children can be helped by a cushion on their lap or a slightly higher chair than usual.

Surface

Reading should take place on a smooth, firm surface. Beginning readers can be helped if a piece of card is placed under the page being read so that dots from the next page or irregularities on the desk top cannot be felt. Most readers will need to read from a firm surface such as a desk top. Even experienced readers, seated in an armchair, are likely to prefer reading a book with a hard cover.

Angle of Book

Care should be taken that the angle of the book to the table top is kept consistent and regularly checked by the child. This ensures that the lines of braille are positioned so that the fingers can sweep along them comfortably and not stray on to adjacent lines.

Reading Schemes

Children learning to read in braille have great difficulty using brailled versions of print reading schemes as there is no control over the introduction of braille contractions and signs. Even the simplest sentence may in print require knowledge of 40–50 signs. One way around this difficulty is to use only the alphabet with beginning braille readers and gradually to introduce the additional braille signs throughout primary schooling. This also allows the child to write any words they wish without being restricted to words whose contraction signs they already know. It also gives them practice in spelling out words which may be important later for typing and computer work. The disadvantages of this approach are that children have to relearn how to write many words, have contraction signs introduced almost as a second language which requires the memorization of rules and sign shapes, may have very slow reading speeds through the laborious process of reading every letter separately, have no access to published literature which helps them through the transition period. Finally, many children can cope with the cognitive load of learning to read and of learning braille simultaneously, and so will have their progress slowed down unnecessarily if each task is taught separately. Most children, therefore, learn to read using specially written schemes in which the reading skills as well as the braille signs are introduced in a controlled systematic fashion. Details of schemes currently available can be obtained from the publishers, Royal National Institute for the Blind. A useful article by Stone (1988) gives guidance on this stage of learning.

Whichever scheme is used, the child will have direct access only to pages of text. The teacher will need to supplement this with the information and experience which is available to sighted children through the pictures in print reading schemes. This visual material may give clues as to the meaning of the text, may be used as a basis for the text or may simply be there to add interest for the child. The teacher of a child using braille material should be mindful of these functions and seek out ways of substituting these experiences using non-visual material. For example, this may involve collecting artefacts associated with places or peoples' jobs as they appear in the stories; using tape-recordings of sound effects or supplementary stories; spending time raising questions about what has happened in a story or prefacing the reading with an overview of the story as would be provided by a picture. These materials and the activities which come from them should not be seen as simply slowing down the process of learning to read. They provide motivation, interest and context which are vital if learning to read is to result in fluent and enthusiastic reading.

Improving Reading

Even with excellent teaching and practice, braille readers are likely to achieve a slower reading speed than print readers – typically 80–100 words per minute (wpm) as opposed to 200–250 wpm. A little research has been carried out into ways of helping children improve their speed of reading although there is not much experience in the UK of systematically developing reading speeds as part of the school curriculum. A useful publication in this area is by Lorimer (1977) who suggests two main types of activities. The first type focuses on the meaning of the text and encourages the use of syntactic and semantic information to anticipate the likely words, phrases or meaning in a passage. This is the same approach as can be used with print reading, but it may well be more critical for a braille reader who might be unable to read efficiently without this extra support. A second type of activity uses many speed reading techniques, substituting the finger for the eyes; skimming, scanning, key words, section headings. For example, as an exercise a reader can try following several lines with several fingers simultaneously. With practice this should enable the reader to make some sense of paragraphs without reading every word. Another exercise involves skimming with just a few seconds on each line. This requires good finger control and the ability to read without feeling the need to examine every word.

Assessment of Braille

Children using braille can have their reading assessed using the same range of parameters as for print reading, but the norms for sighted children cannot be used. Good braille readers will be slower than print readers. This will apply even for silent reading speeds and certainly for using text in which the reader has to answer comprehension questions by finding words or phrases in a passage. The types of mistakes made will also vary and braille mistakes need to be separated from reading mistakes if the assessment is to have a diagnostic function.

The Neale Test of Reading Ability has been produced in braille. This is the only reading test which has a braille version and is based on the original rather than revised version of the Neale Test. Assessment of two aspects of performance in braille is possible using simple tests. Reading speed is critical for successful use of braille and an assessment can identify the likely gap between a reader and sighted colleagues and give evidence from which to consider the need for improvement in reading speed. The Tooze Test of Reading Speed consists of words in braille which do not require the use of braille contractions. The test can therefore be used without knowledge of the braille code interfering with performance. The Lorimer Braille Test consists of lists of words which use all the braille contractions and letter signs. An assessment using this test will identify signs and rules in the braille code which a child has not mastered.

Writing

Braille writing is generally carried out on a Perkins Braille Writer although it can be written on various electronic machines or on a hand frame. The Perkins Writer requires strength in each finger, independent movement of the fingers and coordination of the fingers to operate the keys. Children of pre-school age can usefully spend time at making patterns of dots before starting to use the machine for writing. This is to develop independent movement and strength in the fingers. Other activities involving the fingers – painting, tapping rhythms, screwing, etc. – need to be part of the pre-writing programme. Like typists, good braillists use a specific finger for each key and the earlier this habit can be developed, the more accurate and quick will be the brailling. Children with small hands often have difficulty stretching their fingers across the keys but most children by the age of 6 are able to manage the machine keys and, with practice, can insert the paper correctly by themselves. Two modifications can be made to the machine to help some users. Extension keys can replace the standard keys. These bring all the keys closer together so they may be used with one hand and require less leverage then the standard set-up. A uni-manual model allows one-handed operation by accepting sequential rather than simultaneous input from keys on each side of the braille cell.

Electronic Braille Writers

An overview of the whole range of technology was given in the previous chapter and a number of those machines allow children to write in braille. The output, depending on the machine, will be braille, speech or print. The

Figure 7.2 The Perkin's Brailler in use.
Photo: B. Dallimore, RNIB New College, Worcester.

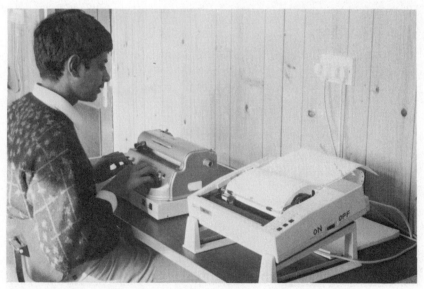

Figure 7.3 This can be linked to an electronic device to produce print.
Photo: B. Dallimore, RNIB New College, Worcester.

devices that are available change rapidly and, throughout the late 1980s, have developed in power of operation and simplicity of use. However, nearly all operate as word-processors with different output systems. Among the considerable advantages they have over the mechanical writer is the ability to edit text.

Some machines have a braille key input, accepting Grade 2 and Grade 1 key combinations. The most long-standing machine of this type is the Versabraille. It has a braille display, is almost silent in operation, can store several hundred pages of text on one disk, allows the writer to search for a word, edit text and output the text as print or braille. The phenomenal power of this technology, particularly in its facility for search and editing, can revolutionize the use of braille for blind people. These facilities overcome two of the three major constraints imposed by mechanical systems and blindness on writing – finding text and editing text (the third constraint was the ability to convert braille into print). The speed of searching for a word, section, or paragraph is now comparable to scanning using the eyes; the ability to edit text, although still nowhere as easy as using a pen, is almost as easy as for print readers using a word-processor (the 20-cell display is a limitation compared to full-screen print display). Of course, the cost of this facility is several thousand pounds as opposed to the cost of a pen, but the introduction of this technology has been as dramatic and innovative as the development of the first mechanical writers earlier in this century.

Figure 7.4 The Versabraille machine is a word-processor with a braille input and output.

Other machines with a braille input have a synthetic speech output. These tend to be very compact machines and are particularly useful for note-taking, with the option usually of transferring information to more sophisticated processors. Some blind people become very adept at using a speech output and find they can manipulate text successfully from spoken commands and information. These small output 'windows' of one word at a time make demands on the user's memory compared to a whole-page display in print or braille and make handling information in tables and graphs particularly difficult.

Braille writing machines with a print output require a translation programme if input is in Grade 2 braille. As this is also needed for a synthetic-speech output, it follows that many of the devices that have a built-in speech output can also be connected directly to a printer to produce a print output and, of course, to a braille embosser to obtain a hard-copy braille version of the text.

All these machines which have keys for a braille input have been made especially for use by blind people and tend to be expensive (although some are now under £1,000). However, computers with standard QWERTY keyboards can operate with synthetic-speech output and be connected to both printers and braille embossers. Programmes are even available to allow keys on the keyboard to function as the keys of a braille machine, storing Grade 2 signs in the memory and outputting these as speech, braille or print. These machines, even with the software, may be considerably less expensive than the special devices and this raises the importance of children being able to use a standard keyboard efficiently. The complexity and size of the keyboard makes it unlikely to be mastered as early as the Perkins machine but children by age 8 or 10 are developing the strength, dexterity and span needed to tackle a keyboard and may well benefit from systematic training from this age.

Despite all these possibilities, some, if not many, braillists prefer a braille display with which they can peruse and examine text. It enables them to read more actively than listening to a speech output and allows them to gain information at a pace they can fully control. The factors of cost, need for access and personal preference will all interact, determining the most appropriate system for an individual.

Tactile Diagram

Tactile representations of drawings are rarely of use to blind children. A line drawing of a tree, for example, consisting of two parallel lines for the trunk and an irregular circular top for the foliage bears no relationship to a child's experience of the texture, shape and sound of a tree. It is so far removed from this experience as to be a separate concept, more distant from reality than for a sighted child. That is not to say that children would not be able to learn to name the shape as a tree. But they may have difficulty relating this symbol to the real object in which different features are critical for their recognition. The presentation of 3-D shapes such as cubes and pyramids in a virtual 2-D form will add extra difficulties and few blind children will be able to understand or use such drawings. Converting visual material into a tactile form requires an understanding of the process of tactile perception, careful consideration of the concepts and information that are being conveyed by the material, and knowledge of and skills in a range of methods of presentation. To understand tactile material, a blind child will need to explore the diagram using learnt techniques of systematic exploration.

The process of tactile perception, as we have seen in earlier chapters, is sequential. A finger tip can cover only one 'finger pad' of information at a time. These separate impressions are then synthesized to form a mental map or image of the shape on the paper. Understanding the spatial relationship between features is particularly challenging and often it is helpful to make diagrams small – certainly no more than one-hand span – so that these relationships can be more easily perceived.

The amount of information that can be understood will usually be much less than can be absorbed through vision and so this will also need to be controlled. The range of potential tactile symbols is smaller than the range of available print symbols and features cannot be placed as close to each other, nor overlapping, as is possible in visual presentation. The types of symbols that can be used in visual or tactile form cover areas, lines and points. A considerable amount of research was carried out in the 1960s into features that made symbols distinguishable from each other. The drawing implements now available through the Royal National Institute for the Blind produce areal, line and point symbols which can be distinguished from each other. From this research came principles such as that lines will be easier to identify if raised rather than incised and broken rather than continuous. Spacing between point symbols should be at least that between dots on a braille cell. Areal symbols will be based on texture rather than height and may need to be used when outlines would be sufficient in print (the finger cannot easily discern if it is within an area if the texture is not different).

Production Techniques

Most tactile diagrams are produced using a vacuum-forming process with a master copy. This master can be made of aluminium foil on to which symbols are drawn using special tools, or it can be made up with card and textured materials (collage method). An alternative method of producing multiple copies uses a special Minolta paper on which black lines are raised up as the paper passes through a stereo photocopier. Simple line drawings can be made on sheets of plastic film especially designed to produce raised lines with a ballpoint pen. All this equipment is available through the RNIB.

Materials that can be used to produce masters for vacuum forming are described in detail by Hinton (1988). They include textured papers and cloths, strings and ribbons, plastic and some metal shapes. Each of these materials can be cut out and stuck to a base sheet to build up a tactile picture. The materials are most satisfactory if they are porous as in the vacuum-forming process; a sheet of plastic is placed over the master copy; the plastic is melted slightly in an oven; a vacuum pump then sucks the plastic sheet over the master copy and, as the sheet cools, it takes the shape of the master. To obtain a clear copy, the pump needs to be able to suck air through all the material so that the plastic sheet is drawn tightly into the shape of the master. An open-weave material, such as rug-making canvas, gives a very sharp, clear texture. Some thicker materials, such as sand-paper, can also be used successfully.

Masters built up in this way are capable of producing many copies without any deterioration of quality and can be stored and used again. But they are time-consuming to make. An alternative quicker method is to use aluminium foil. In this case, the master will crease easily and so is not so suitable for storage. The sheets of foil can be purchased from the RNIB and are thicker than the familiar foil used for cooking. The foil is placed on a rubber backing sheet and indentations made on the surface with specially designed spur wheels or everyday implements such as ballpoint pens and screwdrivers. The sheet can also be placed in a Perkins Brailler if braille text is needed. This should be done, if possible, before lines are drawn, as they may be squashed by the roller on the machine. Of course, because the image is pressed into the foil, it must be drawn in reverse. A pencil drawing on tracing paper is usually made first and then turned over and used to make the tactile master copy. This technique can be used to make fairly accurate diagrams with a wide range of symbols in a short time. The collage method is likely to produce more accurate diagrams with a greater variety of textures and heights and, although they will take longer to produce, they can be filed away for future use.

The Minolta method of production is very simple, using a regular line drawing which is then converted into tactile form by copying it on to special heat-sensitive paper using a Minolta machine. All the markings tend to be the same height and the range of symbols is determined only by the range of markings that can be made with a pen. Each raised line is also printed in black and this can provide a valuable extra clue for those children who have some vision. Some experimental work has been carried out on the computer production of master copies using drawing and painting software packages. In the future, this might well offer the best option for producing tactile material as it is both quick and accurate. At present the cost of the copier and paper is about four times more expensive than vacuum forming and so cost is a factor which might prohibit the development of this method.

It should be remembered that the straight photocopying of a page of print material, for example a page from a maths textbook, through the Minolta process is most unlikely to produce a usable page for a blind child. The text will certainly not be readable and many of the diagrams are likely to be incomprehensible. The page will have to be adapted and redrawn if it is to convey the information in a tactile form.

The 'Sewell' drawing kit, which uses sheets of thin plastic on a rubber backing sheet, is used to make single copies. It produces only one size of line with a ballpoint pen and is most suitable for quick 'sketches' to illustrate a point for a child or for blind children to make diagrams for themselves.

Adapting Material

A suggested sequence for preparing tactile material is as follows:

1. Select medium.
2. Identify educational features and purposes.
3. Eliminate visual/presentational features.
4. Determine number and content of diagrams (e.g. information, symbols, key, accompanying text).
5. Construct diagram(s).

Select Medium

The choice will, first of all, need to take account of the number of copies required and whether the master could usefully be stored for later use. The amount of information to be included and the need for absolute accuracy should then be considered. Other factors, such as the time available to prepare the diagram and the cost of copy, may also have to be considered but, ideally, should be secondary to the educational issues influencing choice.

Identify Educational Features and Purposes

Tactile diagrams usually have to contain less information than visual diagrams and identifying the purpose of the diagram will help in deciding what to include. For example, if a diagram presents a grouping and counting exercise for the child, then the actual examples used may be important (e.g. types of fruit). Changing the example might alter the mathematical difficulty of the exercise and so changes need to be made very carefully. Another diagram, for example, showing heat loss from a house, might indicate a percentage of heat loss through the thickness of arrows and shades of grey. This information is critical to the example but requires no direct deduction from the child and so could be presented in a different form, such as a table. This stage is particularly important in designing maps for mobility. The features that are of help to a blind traveller may be quite different from those needed by a sighted person. A mobility map may contain information about direction of steps, presence of a sound source, slopes, overhanging hazards, as well as regular information required by all travellers. As was noted earlier, some information that is unlikely to transfer into diagrammatic form includes 3-D representations, perspective and geometric figures.

Visual Features
Visual features are identified so that some irrelevant visual features can be identified and eliminated. In our first example, perhaps the head of a smiling child looking at the fruit would be included for visual interest and could be left out of a tactile version to avoid clutter and confusion. In the second example of heat loss in a house, curtains in the windows and bushes in the garden may be drawn in solely to enhance the visual appearance of the picture and so could be left out of the tactile version. However, the teacher would have to make a considered decision as to whether these features were purely ornamental or had been added to see if the sighted child was confused by them or able to use them to help think of answers to questions.

Determine Content
A decision can now be made as to what should be produced. As the information to be included has been identified, the first question is whether it should all go on one diagram or whether several are needed. Many print maps, for example, showing towns, physical features and boundaries would transfer well to three separate maps. If so, each one can be to an identical scale and used a little like overlays on print maps. Sometimes, they can even be constructed back to back so that both hands can be used simultaneously to feel information. The use of keys and accompanying text can also be considered and these are likely to be used far more than with print material. Braille can be produced only in one size and so is a clumsy space-using medium to include on diagrams. The range of symbols should be determined, taking into account the ease of discriminating between adjacent features.

Construction
With aluminium foil, the diagram is drawn on to tracing paper. The paper is reversed and then the foil embossed using a set of point and line tools. The

foil needs to be placed on a rubber mat to ensure that sharp indentations are made that will reproduce clearly on to plastic sheets. The foil need not be pierced but, as a guide, the indentations should feel as clear as a braille dot. If text is to be added to the diagram, it can be written on the foil before embossing the diagram or written on paper which is then stuck on to the foil. Braille should usually be placed parallel to the base of the diagram, particularly if numbers or initials are used, as the cells can have different meanings when placed in different orientations. The thickness of the foil and paper may be too much for the vacuum pump but, if reproduction is poor, pinpricks can be made around the weak area to allow a better suction.

With the collage method, materials need to be selected to contrast with each other and the order in which they will be glued to the base should be established. Care should be taken in selecting material for a background. This will usually be the paper on which the collage is made. If this is the background texture, it should not also be used within the picture. For example, on a map the background sea and land should not be all the same texture, even if a line indicates where the coast is. To the tactile reader, the area under the finger should be clearly identifiable without having to 'see' the rest of the diagram. Throughout the process, the diagram should be judged by its clarity for the finger reader, not for its visual appeal. For young children, the collage method can be used to construct pre-reading and early number exercises. For example, coins can be glued on a sheet of paper or placed directly on the vacuum-forming machine and the resulting copy used in sorting exercises. Plastic or wooden rods, different types of string, grades of sandpaper can all be used to produce sheets of exercises to develop tactile discrimination skills.

Using Tactile Diagrams

Children need to be taught to use tactile diagrams. Tactile discrimination skills will be developed through pre-reading activities. The systematic explanation of diagrams to understand relationships between the features also needs practice. Often, both hands are needed for exploration, with one hand on a fixed point and the other moving out from that point to scan the rest of the area until an accurate picture of the diagram has been built up. The fixed point can be a corner or base of a diagram, the axis of a graph or a central feature on a map. It can change as the diagram is explored for different information.

A final point about the interpretation of all tactile materials. Although a diagram may be clearly reproduced, not contain too much information, be well labelled with a good key, the concepts behind the diagram must be understood by a child. Take, for example, a map in which a number of sites for a settlement are given. The children are asked to suggest which provides the best defensive position. They may understand the map and the questions but, if not fully aware that looking from an island to the mainland is easier than looking down a forested hill, then they may not be able to arrive at the correct answer. Both the preparation and use of tactile material require considerable skill and understanding from the teacher and the child.

The Multi-Handicapped Child

In the preceding section we have been discussing active touch – that is the process of the child using touch to gain information. This is important for all children including those with multi-handicaps. For these children, we also need to examine passive touch – the way in which the child is given tactile experiences by other people. These experiences include massage and co-active ('hands on hands') movement. The adult needs to remember that any physical contact with the child will also be an act of communication and, for some children, an important part of communication. When facial expression and tone of voice are too sophisticated (through learning difficulties) or inaccessible (through sensory impairments), then touch is the primary channel of communication for the child. Information and emotions will be conveyed through touch and so the adult will need to ensure that the intended message is being conveyed. It is easy, for example, for an uneducated, dithering touch to express uncertainty and lack of interest. Communication through touch can express patience, tolerance, affection, impatience and firmness as well as specific requests for action. Effective communication requires careful thought as to how the child is held, pushed, guided, pulled, manipulated and it also requires careful observation of the child's responses.

Providing experiences using passive touch can be described within a framework of tactile environments using the concept of spaces. Children may develop awareness through the following sequence:

* face space;
* body space;
* personal space;
* social space;
* group space.

At the first stage, children's interest centres on their face and experiences tend to involve the tongue, lips and hands near the mouth. Following this early stage, the child's world expands to include the whole body. It is at this stage that many massage activities can be used to create awareness that something is happening to the body. In the third stage, awareness includes the space around the body and objects within that space. These may be people or things and an element of manipulation of these by the child will emerge as an increasing part of the child's activity. The concepts of social and group space refer to an area several feet around the child and to the whole room. The child may start sharing an activity under direction, with another child, and then take part in group activities.

Within this sequence, passive touch will be most important at the first two stages. There are a number of sources of ideas for appropriate activities including publications by Nielsen (1979), McInnes and Treffry (1982), Best (1986), Longhorn (1988). Many of these activities are designed to move a child from a state of unawareness to taking notice of the experiences happening to him. The response of the child is therefore very important in establishing the effect of the experience and a sequence of responses is suggested by McInnes and Treffry (1982).

1. Resist the interaction.
2. Tolerate the interaction co-actively.
3. Co-operate passively.
4. Enjoy the activity.
5. Responds co-operatively.
6. Lead the intervener.
7. Imitate.
8. Initiate the action independently.

Each of these response levels can be converted into a specific behaviour in relation to an activity. Co-operation may be identified, for example, by the stretching of an arm to allow a cloth to be wrapped around it; leading might involve the child taking the intervener's hand and placing it on the vibrator which is giving a sensation. Using this framework, the adult can monitor the development of responses to a particular tactile experience and use this information to judge how much to repeat experiences and when to introduce new ones.

As the child moves through these stages into an awareness of personal space, then the tactile environment extends to the surface on which the child is sitting or lying. Nielsen, a therapist very experienced at working with these children, suggests that a wooden resonance board is a good surface to use at this stage. The board consists of plywood raised about one inch off the ground by a wooden support fastened to the edge of the board. Any movement the child makes can be felt through vibrations on the board and objects dropped or moved on the board will make a clear sound – a 'sound answer' for the child. While valuable, the limitation of this equipment is that it is uni-dimensional. It is only a floor and the walls and ceiling of the room are too far away to be understood by the child. By placing the child in a room about 60 cm high and wide, it is possible for the child to stretch out and touch every side of the space. Neilsen has invented a 'little room' which consists of textured panels made out of wood, fabric, plastic and rubber which can be clipped on to a metal frame to provide a variable environment into which the child can be placed. This environment encourages the child to move, reach and explore by providing a comprehensible space. The child can therefore progress from a stage when passive touch predominates to the beginnings of using active touch. If this environment is kept consistent, it may be particularly helpful for a child who is tactile defensive or does not enjoy touching and being touched. They can control the environment through their own actions of moving, pulling and banging objects. Hard objects with a consistent shape – buckets, plates, wooden spoons – may be preferred to soft objects which confusingly change shape and make little sound – soft toys, sponges, strings of beads. Although there is no research which establishes why some children resist the use of touch, it seems reasonable that success in grasping and controlling the movements of objects may lead to a pleasure in handling them. A carefully constructed environment such as this should present opportunities for this success to be achieved.

Summary

Children who are blind and who have visual impairments will use touch for gaining information. Some children will read and write in braille and, for them, early experiences in using their hands would teach them to be able to recognize braille cells and then develop efficient hand and finger use. Writing braille, previously based on mechanical writing machines, increasingly involves computer technology and children need to be able to handle this equipment so that they can benefit from the greatly enhanced facilities they offer.

Blind children may also gain information through tactile material – graphs, diagrams and maps. The preparation of this material requires an appreciation of the process of tactile perception and a knowledge of the principles of tactile design.

For multi-handicapped children, tactile sensations can help the child move out of a world of isolation and into a world with meaning and success. For these, and other children, touch is likely to provide a medium of communication with other people. Adults need to be conscious of this channel and educate themselves to use it in their interactions with children.

CHAPTER 8

Residual Vision

In Chapter 1 we introduced the definition of clinical assessment of vision. In this chapter we shall examine the assessment of functional vision – the ability to use eyesight in everyday situations – and describe aids to improve the use of functional vision. These aids include both training exercises and the use of equipment. The needs of the child with multi-handicaps for assessment and training are considered in the second part of the chapter.

The differences between clinical and educational assessment were outlined in Chapter 1 when some of the factors affecting use of vision were mentioned. We know, therefore, that seeing an object requires more than clarity of vision ('acuity'). It will require a number of visual skills (e.g. maintaining fixation, changing focus, following a moving object) as well as perceptual skills (e.g. depth perception, visual memory, figure/ground discrimination). It is a combination of these factors working together that we examine in an educational or functional assessment.

How can we establish what a child can see? What situations should we observe? How can we assess if the child is using vision to its full potential? Under what conditions will a child make best use of residual vision?

The material published to help answer these questions can be divided into two main groups. One group of materials is based on a developmental approach. Assessment items are arranged in developmental sequence and any teaching suggestions are designed to move a child through a stage and on to the next level. This approach applies particularly to material developed for use with children who have multi-handicaps. The second approach uses observation of selected situations which are critical to visual functioning. Situations may be for near vision and distance vision. Sometimes this approach provides the observer with a framework which can be applied to any school or child. Jose's book (1983) *Understanding Low Vision* gives very good coverage of both these approaches and is an essential reference for readers wanting to examine this topic in detail.

Near Vision

In the 1960s and 1970s, the work of leading educationalists such as Barraga, Chapman and Tobin, made clear that some aspects of the use of vision could be improved in many children. Research focused on the area of near vision for classroom activities involving printed material. A detailed assessment of the child's visual performance was required. Experienced teachers could then interpret the resulting profile and draw up a programme of training activities. Two main procedures have been devised which examine a child's use of near vision and incorporate suggestions for training programmes. The Diagnostic Assessment Procedure (DAP) is American and consists of an assessment procedure of 40 items and a box of 150 cards containing teaching ideas related to each of the 40 assessment items. The Look and Think Procedure is British and also has an assessment procedure and book of teaching suggestions. It was developed for use with children of approximately 7–11 years of age, although parts of it have been used successfully with children as young as 3 years old. The assessment procedure is divided into 18 areas with four to five items in each area.

In each procedure, the process of seeing has been divided into a number of sub-headings. Research reported in the Look and Think handbook show that the 18 areas of that procedure can be grouped under five main headings. These groupings, like the items in the DAP, 'are based on a rational analysis by professionals in the field of visual handicap as well as by psychologists knowledgeable in the field of visual perception' (DAP Handbook). The groupings, therefore, are not absolute but seemed reasonable to the experienced researchers who devised the materials. The groupings do not have the same names in each procedure, although these frameworks for the systematic observation of significant behaviours cover similar activities, and the information resulting from either could be of help to the teacher.

This information will indicate which items children are able to pass and on which they have failed. But it should also indicate the quality of response. The score sheets have wide margins so that the assessor can note how children perform – if they were hesitant or confident; the distance at which the child worked for different items; the nature of confusions; and so on. In some cases, this information can be as valuable as the profile based on pass/fail scores. The purpose of the procedures is to help develop efficient use of residual vision and for this the assessor has to decide why a child is having difficulty at a visual task. The more information that is available about visual performance, the more precise can be the assessment and subsequent training programme.

There are many reasons why a child might fail an item or area of a procedure. The item might be too demanding intellectually for the child or the language of the instruction too complex. This could be because of lack of educational experiences through missed schooling or because of intellectual impairment. The child might be unable to see the material clearly enough to give a correct answer, either because of lack of acuity or because of inadequate lighting or contrast. The child may lack the visual experiences needed to understand the item, perhaps because of previous discouragement to use vision or because of very poor vision. The child may lack concentration through tiredness, lack of interest or failure of rapport with the assessor. The child may have difficulties because of inefficient use of residual vision – the reason the procedures were initially developed. As can be seen, unravelling the reasons for a child's visual performance and then devising appropriate activities to meet the need for training will require considerable skill and understanding.

Look and Think

The information from these procedures, though, is valuable as it should relate directly to the child's performance in the classroom and provide more detailed information than is available through informal observation. The Look and Think Procedure gives information about 18 separate areas of visual functioning. To illustrate the type of information that might come from this procedure, we shall examine the first few items of this checklist.

The procedure starts with items which use 3-D materials. The child is asked to identify common objects without using touch. He is then asked to name some models. The ability to do this requires adequate visual acuity to recognize the critical features of, for example, a watch and a bracelet. It also requires an understanding of the relationship between a model and the real object, an understanding that is likely to be achieved at a certain developmental level through having had the opportunity to compare, visually, the features of the model and real object.

The third area is concerned with 3-D discrimination. A set of four objects are presented in which one object is slightly different from the others – one cube has rounded edges; one doll has no belt. The child is asked to point to the one that is different. In this task, the reason for the difference is not required, only an awareness that one object is different. To do this, the child requires a multiplicity of skills but one of these is the ability to search and scan across the row of four objects to identify similarities and differences. This systematic scan and search procedure may be particularly difficult if a child has a very narrow field of vision and so can see only part of an object at a time. It may also be difficult if there is a central scotoma blocking out clear macula vision and leaving only indistinct peripheral vision. The child who has not developed an efficient scan and search procedure is likely to jump to a quick but wrong decision about which object is different.

Other parts of this procedure use 2-D material, much of it taken from children's textbooks, to examine an understanding of perspective, line drawings, photographs, facial expressions, patterns and symmetry.

If the assessment profile has identified areas of deficit, the second part of the procedure can be used and this involves devising and carrying out a remedial programme. The Look and Think handbook includes many suggestions for activities which might help strengthen skills in a particular area. Some of these activities use specially devised equipment and details of how this can be made is given in a Teachers' File which accompanies the handbook. Other activities use regular educational equipment although sometimes the instruction and visual demands of the task can be altered to emphasize the visual skills being developed. For example, fitting together a jigsaw of a face can be organized to help develop scan and search techniques if the pieces are spread over a table and the child expected to find them all. The same equipment can be used to identify critical features if the puzzle is nearly completed by the adult and the child is then handed the last few pieces, one at a time, and asked to guess where each piece might fit.

Vision Aids

Many aids to low vision are used in near-vision tasks. As was outlined in Chapter 6, low-vision optical aids and CCTV are useful for many children and can be used in examining pictures, graphs, maps and diagrams as well as in reading and writing. The key to successful use is proper training and, although some children can use these aids efficiently after a brief explanation of their features, most children will need a series of training sessions in which they learn about the capabilities of the aid and master its use at a variety of tasks. In the case of children who are initially reluctant to use the aid because of self-consciousness, this training may give them the confidence to try out its use in class.

The term 'low-vision aids' is used for any aid made up of a lens or series of lenses. They are usually used to magnify the image of what is being looked at. The degree of magnification is fixed by the power, or shape, of the lens. The working distance of the lens – the distance of the eye from the lens and the lens from the paper – is also fixed as a characteristic of a lens. For higher-powered lenses this distance will be critical, with a very small range over which a focused image can be obtained. The field of view of a lens is also defined by its power, or magnification, with the stronger lenses having a smaller field of view. Lower-powered lenses, therefore, allow for more flexibility in use.

Different types of lenses are available for near-vision work. A common type, which can be purchased without prescription in the UK, is the stand magnifier. A single lens is mounted on a stand which fixes its distance from the object to be viewed. It can therefore be used easily by primary-school-aged children who do not have the problem of finding and maintaining the correct working distance relative to the object viewed. Some of these magnifiers have built-in battery-powered illumination. Hand-held magnifiers are less bulky and are available with the same range of powers as stand magnifiers but do need to be held steadily at the correct working distance and so tend to be most appropriate for use over a short period, for example, to check a label, title, wall-mounted timetable and so on. Spectacle-mounted aids are commonly prescribed for children who can benefit from magnification for reading and writing. They may consist of a lens or series of lenses for one eye as there are often problems in using the images from both eyes together. A very high degree of magnification over a small field is possible with these lens systems.

CCTV are non-optical LVAs; that is they consist of a camera and television set rather than lenses. They can give a much greater degree of magnification than a lens, the quality of the image can be changed using the TV controls, and viewers can adjust their distance from the screen in order to see the image most clearly. However, CCTVs are very bulky and even the portable models would be too heavy for most primary-aged children. They require an electric socket and are very much more expensive than lenses. Most systems only work with black-and-white television screens.

Choice of Aids

An optical LVA can only be prescribed, in the UK by an appropriately qualified medical practitioner. However, educationalists are often involved in this decision and will certainly be largely responsible for subsequent use of the aid by the child. Factors affecting the choice of aid will start with cost, but other factors will include requirements of the visual condition, purposes and uses of aid, motor and cognitive ability to master the use of the aid and motivation.

The visual condition will determine whether magnification might be of help, the level of magnification needed and will influence the lighting conditions for optimum viewing. A major consideration in use of the aid would be its portability, particularly in secondary schools where children will move between many rooms during a day. If an aid is needed for writing, there must be space for the pen between the lens and paper. This is no problem with some CCTV systems but may not be possible with some lenses. If colour vision, for map work, for example, is important, then many CCTV systems would not be appropriate, but it may be easier to see the spatial relationships on a screen rather than use an optical aid with a small field of view. The motor skills needed to use a hand-held aid and some stand magnifiers make them difficult for children under the age of 7, but by no means impossible. The electronic and platform controls on most CCTV systems may also be difficult for young children to master. In practice, motivation seems to be the most important factor affecting use of aids. Self-consciousness about the aid is probably the major cause of under-use of aids which have been prescribed as potentially useful. More detailed information about types of aids and their use can be found in chapters in *Understanding Low Vision* by Jose (1983).

Training

The content of a training programme has never been established but the following suggestions will provide a framework which should cover most of the skills needed.

For the use of optical aids, children will need practice in:

* scanning print material to locate sections;
* following a line of text;
* focusing a clear image;
* developing speed and fluency of use;
* using any controls (e.g. batteries, auxiliary lens);
* using the aid at a range of appropriate tasks;
* cleaning, maintaining and caring for the aid;
* developing a good posture during use.

For CCTV, all of the above will apply and, in addition, the following techniques will be needed:

* Camera Controls
  - print size;
  - focusing;
  - zooming;
  - aperture.

- Screen Output
  - contrast;
  - brightness;
  - positive/negative image;
  - split screen and line marker;
  - use with interfaces;
  - platform.
- Position of Work
  - movements of work on platform;
  - use of margins.

Although in this section we are concerned with near vision, it should be noted that both optical aids and CCTVs can be used for distance viewing and training will include applying these techniques to distance tasks as well as in near-vision situations.

For all of these skills, children will be helped by explanations, experimentation and practice. Teachers may find it helpful to build up a collection of different types of print material, including text, text in columns, line drawings, comics, coloured and black-and-white pictures, graphs, maps, text with pictures. It may also be useful to prepare passages with different size and style of print. This could be used to give the child practice in reading different styles and in learning to adjust the controls between different passages. Establishing the optimum size and magnification for a CCTV, though, cannot be achieved by reading short passages and may need several days' usage before a decision can be made about the best settings. Some children are helped by the use of line markers. These may be thick lines drawn on the left-hand margin of a page or a piece of coloured card which can be held above or below a line of print or at the beginning of a line. These help in the location of text.

A quite different approach to training at near-vision tasks has been developed and published by Backman and Inde (1982) from Sweden. The basis of their work is to encourage viewing techniques according to the type of visual defect that the person suffers from. They divide defects into four main types and provide exercises using print, appropriate for each condition. Those people with central scotoma (or opacities in the centre of their field of vision) are encouraged to use eccentric viewing techniques. This involves looking slightly above or below a line of print in order that the image is received on an undamaged part of the retina. With practice, a 'secondary macula' develops with the brain taking information from this image and analysing it to recognize the letter or word. For sufficient information to be received in the visual cortex, a large number of retinal cells needs to be stimulated. The print, therefore, is often magnified so that the image falls over a large area of the retina. People with nystagmus are encouraged to find the position of their eyeball in its socket at which least eye movement takes place and then to move the book and head, rather than the eyes, so that the position is maintained. Peripheral restrictions and narrow fields of vision can be helped by small letters and increasing the size of the fixation span. Exercises help the eyes to move more efficiently along lines of print. These exercises seem to be particularly successful with people who lose some of their vision, but they may also help children with congenital visual impairments. Details of the groups and exercises are included in their book.

Distance Vision

At the beginning of this chapter, it was suggested that assessment procedures could be grouped as developmental-based and as situation-based. In assessing distance functional vision, nearly all procedures use a situation-based approach. The range of general situations can be defined, although teachers will want to draw up their own list for a child in a specific school. Models for checklists can be found in the work of Barraga (in the Diagnostic Assessment Procedure) and in Jose (1983).

Most checklists include indoor and outdoor activities. The indoor situations will cover the child's performance in different rooms, for example, classroom, dining room and gym, and they will also include performance when the child is sitting as well as when moving about, including in the foyer, corridors and on the stairs.

A complete assessment will compare the child's performance in familiar and unfamiliar situations. The task of recognizing a familiar object in the context in which it is expected is far easier, visually, than identifying an unknown object in a strange situation. Locating a door handle, for example, a doorway or a new notice on a bulletin board may all be possible with very low levels of vision, if the task is simply to pinpoint the object in the expected location. If the task, though, is to identify a blurred shape without knowing what to expect, as in recognizing the features of an unknown person, a higher level of visual acuity is needed. This is particularly so if the context does not provide a strong clue.

In outdoor situations, the assessment should cover a full range of locations and tasks in which the child will want to function. This will include playground, areas between school buildings, streets, junctions, shopping centres, open spaces such as car parks and parkland. The tasks the child will engage in will depend on the age and ability of the child but could include:

- Crossing roads using kerbs, traffic islands, traffic lights, judging traffic speed.
- Identifying buildings, roadsigns, bus stops, street furniture.
- Using public transport, identifying buses, finding a seat, knowing when to alight.

An interesting exploratory framework for observing children in both indoors and outdoor situations has been suggested by Hyvarinen (1985). This is designed as a framework for defining a child with visual impairments but would serve as the starting point for assessment. Four types of activities are identified and for each of these the child's performance is assessed as being a blind child, partially sighted or visually normal child. Developments in this procedure may show that different eye conditions produce characteristic profiles (compare, for example, cataract, retinitis pigmentosa, macula degeneration.)

Table 8.1 Classification of visual impairments

	Blind	*Partial sight*	*Visually normal*
Orientation and mobility			
Activities of daily living			
Communication			
Sustained near work			

In both indoor and outdoor situations, the assessor will want to observe what the child can do and how he does it. Factors such as speed, accuracy, anticipation and confidence will need to be noted as well as the use of aids. Where a child is having difficulty, the cause could be lack of acuity, lack of experience or lack of visual efficiency. Lack of experience can be helped by giving graded exercises to develop a specific skill. Lack of visual efficiency requires a training programme aimed at the use of vision to better effect. Some of the skills needed are the same as used in near vision – scan and search, recognizing critical features. For example, a child with a narrow field of vision might be encouraged to locate the junction of stairs with a side wall where the contrast helps in seeing the shape of the steps. Other skills are more specific to distance viewing – using body movement to detect figure/ground differences, understanding what is happening by integrating sound and visual information, using visual edges in flooring and between floors and walls to identify areas and direction. Further information about training for distance vision can be found in Jose (1983).

Children with Severe Learning Difficulties

Assessment

The process of assessing and developing residual vision in children with severe learning difficulties received a great deal of attention during the 1980s and many ideas were tried out. Only a little of this work has been evaluated and therefore many suggestions that can be given are largely based on experience and observed practice rather than being distilled from evaluated practice and research.

The two approaches to assessment – developmental- and situational-based – which were outlined at the beginning of this chapter, apply also to work with children with severe learning difficulties. The developmental approach focuses on the very early stages in the development of vision and this involves five major stages:

- awareness;
- fixation;
- tracking;
- changing focus;
- visual exploration.

At the level of visual awareness the child is learning that it is possible to see that images in the head relate to real objects 'out there'. This stage is followed by development of fixation, the ability to look at an object and keep the eyes fixed on it – to 'see' the object. Tracking involves following an object and there are many different directions and distances over which this ability can be used. If children can move their gaze from one object to another, they are at the fourth stage of those listed above. The action is led by the attention of the child and requires visual memory as well as physical skills such as moving the eyes and focusing images at different distances. Visual exploration requires systematic searching over a field of vision to identify critical features in objects in order to identify them.

Each of these stages can be broken down into a number of sub-stages and this would then provide one form of assessment checklist. For example, tracking can be divided into movements from the midline outwards to the left, right, up and down; from the edge of the visual field in, from each direction, to a mid point; diagonal movements; movement across the whole field of vision; movements from a near point outwards and in the opposite direction. Amongst the published literature which uses this approach is a comprehensive manual by Langley (1981) which also contains ideas for activities which can help a child move from one stage to the next. A useful handbook by Smith and Cote (1982) contains an assessment procedure and some ideas for follow-up activities.

A different developmental sequence has been suggested by Bell (1986). Her sequence starts with a stage of visual *bombardment* in which the child can be exposed to a wide range of visual experiences but will not yet have developed a preference for specific stimuli or viewing conditions. The next stage is of *assessment* in which the child is beginning to develop visual preferences, and observation of visual performance will enable the observer to identify these. The process of visual stimulation is still part of the curriculum content. At the next stage, looking is used by the child as a method of access to experiences. This third stage of *teaching* involves giving a programme of visual stimulation to the child and, in the fourth stage, the skills learnt would be applied to daily situations in a process of *generalization*.

For children at a very early developmental stage, two procedures may help in establishing how much a child can see. Firstly, a conditioned response can be built up with a visual stimulus. An easily seen object is presented to the child and then a response noted or introduced. The object, a brightly coloured ball for example, can be moved near the child's face and then the child is tickled. After many repetitions of this activity the ball can be presented and, if the child shows signs of anticipating the tickle, it can be deduced that the ball has been seen.

Different objects can be used to build up an idea of the range of vision that is present. These stimulus objects can be varied according to three variables: distance of presentation, size of object, visual clarity (that is, the extent to which the object stands out from its background). The response to the stimulus can also be varied. Any action which is pleasant for the child or which produces a response can be introduced, such as a tickle or blowing in the child's eye to make it blink. The stimulus object itself can create a response as with rolling a large ball towards the child so that the child anticipates the ball by holding out his hands.

Some 'practice' will be needed before the child's brain can make a link between the stimulus object and its consequence. The number of repetitions required can be tested using a tactile stimulus, say tapping on the tummy. If three five-minute 'practice' sessions are needed before a child anticipates the tickle, then this gives a rough guide as to the amount of practice that will be needed before a visual stimulus produces a response. If, after this amount of practice, there are no signs of anticipation, then it can be tentatively assumed that the object has not been seen. What happens is an almost subconscious reflex that occurs, rather than a deliberate action by the child.

The presentation of the object has to be carried out carefully. It should be moved into view at irregular time intervals so that a rhythm of presentation does not alert the child to what is about to happen. The presentation should not be accompanied by other clues – sound, wind on the child's face, the shadow of the presenter's arm lowering the temperature on the face, a scent as the presenter moves close to the child. Of course, these extra clues can be used, if necessary, to make the object easier to locate – a squeaky toy might alert the child to the object and encourage the movement of the eyes towards the object – but these clues will then need to be eliminated if a reliable assessment of vision is to be achieved.

A second procedure, called preferential looking, has been developed by Atkinson and Braddick (1979) (see p. 13). It requires the child to show a preference between two stimulus objects and an observer notes the child's eye movement as the objects are presented. This procedure was first developed for use with young babies who can be assessed using cards with a grid pattern of different thicknesses of line and in varying degrees of grey. The principles of the procedure can also be used with various-sized white balls on a black background, lights of different brightness, toys of different colours or moving and stationary objects.

The use of situation-based checklists is more complex with this group of children, as there is a wide range of abilities within the group. Yet it is clearly of help to be able to identify the child's performance in relation to specific situations where the level of motivation may be different (and yet critical) as well as to the visual demands of the environment and activities. Perhaps the most useful approach is to identify the variables which will affect performance and provide a framework for observation which can be applied to any child. A suggestion for this framework is given below.

The variables in terms of what is seen were identified in the previous section. They were the *distance* of the object, and in particular the furthest distance at which a specific object is seen; the *size* of the object and, in particular, the smallest object that can be seen; the visual *clarity* of the object – the extent to which the object stands out from its background. Three types of background present different levels of visual clarity: a background which contrasts strongly with the stimulus object, a plain background which may not be of high contrast with the object and a patterned background into which the object may merge. The observations should establish the child's visual threshold for each of these three variables. This will not necessarily be the limits of the child's visual ability but will be the extent to which the child is using available vision. The process of assessment must be linked to teaching and, having established a visual threshold, the adult can then encourage the child to see more by providing graded opportunities for using vision. Suggestions for this are discussed in the next section.

The activities which are observed will depend on the individual child, but it is suggested that they should cover tasks at three zones of vision: near vision – on a table top at 1 to 2 feet; middle distance – about 6 to

8 feet from the child; far distance – across a room. And at each of these distances, observations should be made of familiar and unfamiliar situations. This is particularly important for children with additional handicaps as the ability to interpret visual images requires the use of context clues, past experiences and co-ordination with other sensory information. In an unfamiliar situation, using this information may be particularly difficult for children with learning difficulties and so the difference between visual performance in familiar and unfamiliar situations may be very marked. This framework, then, can provide a basis for assessment and teaching. Examples of this in practice can be found in a training video produced by Sense which is titled 'Using Residual Vision'.

When children's use of vision is being observed, at least three main aspects of their behaviour can be noted. Each one can lead to deductions about a child's vision.

- Visually Directed Reach
  - accuracy
  - confidence
  - fluency
  - speed

(These apply to hand movements and, for children who can walk, to foot movements.)

- Viewing Posture
  - position of eyes (use of both eyes, use of central or peripheral vision);
  - position of head;
  - viewing distance;
  - length of time in exploration.

- Use of Touch
  - after viewing – to check what is being viewed;
  - before viewing – to locate objects to be viewed;
  - in combination with vision instead of vision.

A further approach to assessment of residual vision is suggested by Corn (1983). She proposes a model of visual functioning in which she identifies a comprehensive list of factors affecting our ability to see and groups these into three main headings, visual abilities; environmental cues; stored and available individuality. Failure to see an object or action may be the result of deficiencies in any of these variables and the assessor can consider which is likely to be relevant to the situation and child under examination and can therefore make appropriate changes to the situation, presentation or activity.

Stimulation of Vision

The processes of assessment and teaching are completely dependent on each other and one cannot reasonably take place without the other. Visual assessment is likely to lead to hypotheses about what the child can see which are then tested through a programme of stimulation activities. These activities may well result in the child learning to use the residual vision more efficiently and so these lead to reassessment and then further activities.

Stimulation activities need to be appropriate in interest level and in visual clarity. A distinction should be made between activities which train the child to look and those in which the child has to look to complete the activity. For example, a common activity to stimulate early looking is to move a coloured torch in front of the child while turning the light on and off. The purpose would be to encourage the child to fixate on the light and, perhaps, even to follow it. The light will be easy to see if it is moved against a dark background (visual clarity) and it is assumed that a coloured light is interesting for the child (interest level). The reward for the child is to see the light, and progress is measured by noting an increase in the length of time the child stays looking at the light. Seeing the light will bring pleasure and so, eventually, the child will be encouraged to look at other objects. Such an activity fits in well to Bell's stage of Visual Bombardment outlined earlier.

An alternative activity, which may well present the same level of visual difficulty, is to link looking at a light with the *onset* of a reward such as some flashing lights, a few seconds' blast of warm air from a hair-drier or some music. The torch is flashed on and off, as before, but the child's act of looking at the light will produce the response. In this case, the child is using vision to complete the activity – is looking for a purpose, not just for pleasure. The extra cognitive element of linking the two activities will be within the capability of most children who are at the stage of searching and fixating on an object and it could be that the motivation to look in this activity will make it more likely to produce results than in the former activity in which the child has no apparent control nor influence over what is happening.

Objects that are easy to see, like bright lights, will be an important part of the materials used in visual stimulation. However, the interest level of these materials may not be as high as, for example, a wind-up toy which moves vigorously (or something the child can eat or drink). If both can be seen by the child, it may well be that the toy would encourage looking more than the light. The stimulation activity could be structured as follows. A wind-up dog with legs that move could be held in front of the child at a distance at which the child should be able to see it (this is unlikely to be closer than about 8 inches). If the child looks at the dog, the adult lets it move for a few seconds. The noise and movement should encourage the child to continue looking. After a few seconds the dog is moved out of vision and then brought back again and the activity repeated. An extension of this activity involves an extra element of hand–eye co-ordination in which the movement of the dog is consequent on the child touching a pad, the arm of a wheelchair, the adult or a switch. The child has to use vision to locate the 'trigger' and then obtains a visual (or multi-sensory) reward for the action. Lists of appropriate materials for visual stimulation are included in the books already referred to by Langley (1981) and in an excellent chapter in the book by Longhorn. The newsletter, *Information Exchange*, from the Royal National Institute for the Blind also contains many excellent ideas for materials and activities.

As well as activities aimed specifically at developing use of vision, the general teaching approach can encourage use of vision. Objects can be held in front of the child and time given for the child to reach for them. An object to be picked up can be tapped on the table to alert the child who is then encouraged, with physical help if necessary, to locate it visually and grasp it. Opportunities can be created for the child to look. For example, at mealtimes, the adult can hold a cup in front of the child and give time for the child to look at it before bringing it to the child's lips. A flannel to wipe the child's mouth can be slowly brought near the child and the child given time to anticipate what is going to happen, by visually locating and touching the flannel, before it is placed on his face.

The Environment

Activities to develop the use of vision can take place in a regular classroom but there may be advantages to using a special visual stimulation area, or 'dark room', in which the lighting and contrast is controlled and in which there are fewer distractions. Some of the elements of a good visual environment were outlined in Chapter 4. In a dark room the decor and equipment can be selected to provide the best possible surroundings for the child. The following elements need consideration in setting up a special visual environment:

- Decor
  - walls;
  - floor;
  - ceiling.
- Lighting
  - overhead;
  - task;

  - ultra-violet;
  - switches.
- Equipment
  - electronic;
  - non-electronic;
  - multi-sensory.

Decor
A room for visual stimulation should be big enough to hold one adult and a child easily and preferably at least two adults and two children. The decor needs to be as plain as possible and walls, ceiling and floor should be of plain colours. A dark, matt finish is best to reduce reflections and glare. Black is a good colour, particularly if ultra-violet light is to be used, as this needs a totally dark environment to be effective, although a dark blue or green would also be perfectly satisfactory. If the room is to be used as a pleasant relaxing area, as well as for intensive work, a dark colour might be preferred. An alternative is to have one wall of a lighter colour, or white, and a full-length black curtain to pull across it. This gives the flexibility to use projectors and create a brighter area when desired.

Natural light should be eliminated from the room by blocking out any window completely. Without natural ventilation, there must be adequate control of heating and a fan, if quiet, could be essential.

Lighting
Lighting should be flexible with each overhead fitting on a separate switch. Fluorescent tubes will be more effective if used with baffles which diffuse the light and reflected light will give a more even illumination than direct light from the ceiling. Table lamps can be positioned to bounce light off a wall or give pools of strong light, but they will need to be secured on table surfaces, floor stands or wall brackets, and the leads should be kept safely out of the child's way. Ultra-violet lighting can be superb for helping children see but the type and position of these lights is critical and is dealt with in a later section.

If all lights are controlled through dimmer switches, then the adult can create the visual effect most suited to the activity and the needs of each child.

Equipment
Projectors can be used with oil-filled slides to create dramatic visual effects involving colours and movement. They allow the child to be bathed in light and influence the shape and atmosphere of the whole environment. Technology such as light tubes, fibre optics and low-powered lasers can be used, although simpler technology, such as a torch

and mirror, can also give interesting effects for children. Computers, for some reason, have a powerful effect on many children and have been used most successfully for stimulation, using patterns of flashing and moving colour, and for more complex discrimination tasks. Some devices link sight with sounds. The volume of the music, the child's voice or sounds the child makes control the brightness of lights, while the pitch of the sound controls which lights turn on. This equipment is common in discos and is available in portable units.

Non-electronic equipment will be equally important for stimulating vision and the literature referred to above will give many ideas for equipment and activities.

These special areas can be for activities other than stimulation of vision. A multi-sensory environment, in which vision, sounds, smell, temperature, air movement and tactile experiences are all available, may be of help to children with visual impairments. As they have particular difficulties in finding opportunities to control the environment, understand the relationships between cause and effect and receive clear feedback from their actions, an environment such as that provided by the Snoezelen concept, at de Hartenberg in Holland, may be particularly valuable.

The Snoezelen environment can be described as a multi-sensory environment. A series of rooms have been created in which light, sounds, smells and tactile sensations can all be experienced. For example, handicapped people can watch tubes of bubbles, changing patterns of lights projected on to white walls, lights that turn on in response to noises made by the person. Floors may have panels of different coloured lights, each with a different temperature. Flexible tubes can be turned on by touching different switches to make them blow scented air. This type of environment can give some handicapped people the opportunity to receive pleasant or exciting stimulation while being in control of what happens, although a staff member may still be needed to assist and enable the person to achieve the experiences.

Ultra-violet (UV) Lighting

UV light, or black light as it is sometimes called, can cause certain objects to fluoresce. It is this quality that results in its use in discos and in theatres where dramatic effects can be achieved through the use of special paints and certain clothing material. A range of plastic toys and common objects also fluoresce under UV lighting and this is particularly noticeable where there is no other source of light in a room and where the walls, ceiling and floor are black.

Why is UV lighting suggested as a useful aid in working with children who have learning difficulties? Very little indeed has been written about this, but practical experience, reports from teachers and the sparse literature suggest that there are four major reasons. One claim is that it helps children to see as the light is so bright. The high level of light reflected from fluorescent materials can enable children with low level of vision to see colours and shapes which they cannot discern in white light. The brightness may also help those who can see under regular lighting conditions to see more clearly. Secondly, the heightened contrast makes fluorescing objects stand out with more visual clarity. The non-fluorescing background appears black in sharp contrast to the bright objects which fluoresce. This again results in objects' being easier to see. Thirdly, the attractive bright colours may result in increased interest in looking at objects and, with the very low levels of interest found in many children with learning difficulties, gaining the child's interest is an important factor. Fourthly, the lack of visual distractions may result in improved attention.

Some teachers and therapists who have used UV lighting in the UK and in the USA are enthusiastic about the results. Children have been observed to peer as if they were looking for the correct shape before picking it up and putting it in the sorting box; children may reach directly for an object and pick it up neatly rather than fumbling over the table top to look for it; children with very poor vision have responded to colours and lights for the first time under UV lights; children have been able to make and see their own drawings for the first time under UV lights; children have shown good tracking and fixating skills which they did not exhibit in regular lighting; children have sat on a chair for several minutes in UV lighting, while appearing unwilling to do so in regular lighting. One cannot discount these incidents, although one would naturally want to try to separate the effect of UV lighting from the effect of an enthusiastic teacher.

Safety

The major difficulty with UV lighting is that it is potentially hazardous and can cause damage to the skin and eyes if received in sufficiently large doses. In the UK, there are recommendations for the maximum exposure to UV lighting that are permitted, and so it should be possible to calculate the limits of safe use. However, sensitivity to the harmful effects can be heightened in those taking certain medications and so there may be uncertainty about its use with some children.

What is UV light and what are the potential hazards? What is generally called UV light is radiation emitted below the visible spectrum in the 100–400 nanometer (nm) wavebands (nanometers are units of measurement-of-light wavelengths). It can be divided into three types according to lengths and each type has different properties.

UVA light (315–400 nm) is the least dangerous and is the type responsible for making objects fluoresce. It is sometimes called 'black light'. Over-exposure might result in a temporary darkening of the skin and there is a possibility that it may be involved in the development of certain types of cataract, but this possibility has not been fully investigated. UVB (280–315 nm) and UVC (100–280 nm) light is much more dangerous, causing damage to the cornea of the eye, 'sunburn' and, in extreme cases, cancer of the skin. However, it is important to state that this occurs only after extremely heavy exposure. We are all familiar with the effects of mild exposure, as it can occur in sunlight and causes reddening, thickening and then a desirable tanning of the skin.

Safe exposure times are calculated in terms of wavelengths, output and distance of viewing. Most lamps emit only a very small amount of light in the most harmful wavelengths. For the combined UVA, UVB and UVC wavelengths, the commonly available 8-W tubes should be within the safety recommendations when used at 20 inches for up to 4 hours in an 8-hour period. At 5 feet, the amount of irradiation is so slight they can be used continuously within an 8-hour period. The more powerful 40-W 4-feet tubes can be used at 5 feet for 4 hours in an 8-hour period and for 8 hours at a distance of 7 feet (these figures have been obtained by the author from three independent university safety departments).

The recommended safety limits should ensure that no damage can be caused by radiation. However, individuals do vary as to their sensitivity to radiation and these variations may be largely due to skin pigmentation, although many other factors, including taking tranquillizers which contain photo-sensitizing elements, will have an influence. Some people, for example, find that several minutes' exposure can cause a headache, even though exposure is well within the recommended limits. There are, however, several precautions which can be taken to provide sensible protection against harmful radiation.

Distance. The power of radiation falls off very dramatically with increased distance and so the working area should be as far away as possible from the lamp.

Decor. Glossy and light-coloured surfaces tend to reflect UV light and so radiation can be reduced by using dark matt surfaces. A room with black walls, ceiling and carpet will ensure efficient use of the UV light available. This decor will also ensure that contrast will be at maximum and so only low levels of UV light will be required.

Diffusion. Concentrations of light can be avoided by using fluorescent striplights rather than bulbs. Even better than one 4-foot tube could be two shorter 8-W tubes placed some distance apart They would still provide adequate light for an area 6–8 foot square but would avoid the higher levels of radiation often found directly under a tube.

Shielding. Lights should be shielded from direct viewing by being positioned pointing to the ceiling or at an angle where the tube cannot be seen. This will avoid the highest concentrations of light. Perspex acts as a barrier to harmful light and so can be used for protection.

Clothing. UV light has very low power of penetration and is generally absorbed by clothing material which does not fluoresce. Appropriate clothing, including thin gloves can therefore protect nearly all the body except the face.

Timing. Activity sessions should be of short duration – say 5–10 minutes. This should be a safe period of time as well as being educationally satisfactory.

Activities
Most activities which could help children under regular lighting conditions can also be tried out in UV light. The following suggestions give an indication of the range of possibilities. In each case, the objects will need to be of fluorescent material:

Looking. Rolling tennis balls, bouncing tennis balls fastened with elastic, wind-up toys (e.g. drummer, jumping dog).

Watching hands (own or adults). With paper stickers on fingernails, with plasticine 'rings' on fingers, with sock or glove.

Searching. Tape-recorder 'on' switch (with sticker or dab of paint), finding objects covered with black cloth, posting box (shapes and edge of posting holes outlined).

Drawing. Felt-tip pens, crayons, stencils, handwriting.

Further information about the use of UV lighting with handicapped children has been published by Poland and Doebler (1980) and by Potenski (1983). Boyce (1981) discusses the characteristics of UV lighting in his textbook *Human Factors in Lighting* and the National Radiological Protection Board publishes safety guidelines through the HMSO.

Summary

One of the the main tenets in this field of education is the importance of developing the use of residual vision. By assessing levels of functional vision and, where appropriate, providing a programme of vision training, many children can be helped to make better use of the vision they possess.

Approaches to assessment can be based on a developmental sequence or on the observation of a child's use of vision in a number of everyday situations. The Look and Think procedure is currently the most comprehensive assessment and training package available and this focuses on the child's use of vision for near tasks.

For some children, their use of vision can also be assisted by low-vision aids. Whatever the type of aid, children are likely to need help in learning to use the aid efficiently.

Children with additional impairments also seem able to benefit from stimulation in their use of vision, although the research evidence for this is sparse. Again, programmes need to be based on careful assessment, carried out through teaching and over time. Stimulation activities may be most successfully carried out in a controlled visual environment. The use of ultra-violet lighting within such an environment may produce good results, but the potential hazards of the lighting mean it must be used with care.

CHAPTER 9

Listening Skills

We have already outlined the importance of sounds to children with visual impairments. In this chapter we shall examine in more detail the situations in which sounds or verbal information may be important for a child with visual impairment. We shall then discuss the skills needed by adults to present high-quality useful verbal information. This includes preparing and using tape-recorded information. Finally we shall discuss ways in which children can be helped to develop listening skills and to use verbal information.

In Chapter 1 we read of the young girl beginning to discover the meaning of 'see'. In that situation she seemed to be trying to understand how adults (she may also be thinking of 'sighted people') use the word 'see' and comparing it with her concept of 'in contact with'.

Nielsen (1988) tells the story of a severely partially sighted child, back in the classroom, having spent the morning on a farm where he saw a range of animals and machinery. The children are drawing pictures of the experience and this boy has scribbled vigorously with a red crayon in the centre of the paper. 'Tell me about your picture,' the teacher asks, 'what is this?' pointing at the red scribble. 'Why, that is a tractor,' says the child, 'can't you hear it?' The child is re-living the experience in his terms, using sound information.

Both these examples illustrate the central position that sounds and words may have for the child with visual impairment. To use this information efficiently requires good listening skills. But what exactly are these skills and when will they be used? Listening can be used for speech and for environmental sounds. Both aspects are discussed here.

From the earliest stages, the sounds of speech will be used by children to help identify the speaker. Later, the words themselves will be an important source of information to supplement the children's own visual or tactile experiences. Sounds, at this early stage, will provide information and interest. They will help children maintain contact with their surroundings as they come to understand that there is an 'out-there'. Sound information will be used to understand concepts of position and direction such as in front of, above, further away from. Sound information will help in knowing what objects are around and what is happening – that someone is approaching with a bowl of food and who it is; that the child has crawled near a radio; that the cupboard door has been opened and pots are being taken out of it.

During school years, the spoken word will become of prime importance as a source of information, particularly as learning becomes based on more abstract concepts during later primary and secondary years. In listening to speech, the child will have to extract critical information through concentration and selective listening. Sound information will continue to provide important clues as to what is happening and where the child is. Much of this information is related to mobility and to the child's ability to be orientated in its surroundings. This will involve skills such as sound identification and location, use of sound shadows and echo location.

The use of listening skills may present a particular challenge to children who have recently lost all or part of their vision. They may not know how to interpret sound information and will certainly have some difficulty in concentrating on listening for extended periods of time. Typically, they will seem to be day-dreaming, may forget things that have been explained to them, may seem to become easily tired at school. They may even develop apathy, lack of confidence, very quiet speech and be startled when people talk to them. Children at this stage often need some specific help in listening so that they can efficiently process information and develop the specific skills mentioned towards the end of the chapter.

In helping children, adults working with very young children need to recognize that the child may still and stiffen when listening. This action can sometimes be misunderstood when children stiffen as an adult approaches them. Children will be helped to anticipate activities if given sound information about what is happening. For example, tapping the spoon on the side of a bowl or saying 'Here it comes,' as the loaded spoon is moved up to the mouth. The child can be given some verbal information about what is happening. This should not be a constant nor detailed commentary, but rather provide selected pieces of information to reassure and inform the child – perhaps pointing out if an adult is leaving or entering a room; a comment alerting the child to a noise such as a radio that is going to be switched on; an explanation of a noise such as dropping a pan lid on a work surface or a bottle of shampoo in the bath.

Adults also need to be aware that totally blind children will usually be able to reach in response to sounds between the ages of 1 and 2, but that this is considerably later than sighted children develop visual directed reaching. There can be no direct substitution of sound for visual information and children may need physical help to locate objects through sound, both in reaching and moving. This physical help may be through holding the child's hand or wrist or through standing in front of the child and guiding the child to the object.

Adults can also help the development of the child's use of language through providing the child with encouragement and opportunities to ask and answer questions. Sometimes blind children do ask a lot of questions but do not always need to know the answer. These questions can be used to make and maintain contact with their surroundings – to check what is 'out there' and to help the children know they are still being noticed.

Guidelines on the use of voice and giving clear verbal information were given in Chapter 5. This applies to children of pre-school and of school age. These guidelines include the suggestion that children be given the opportunity to attend to sounds, particular speech, through having some kind of alerting signal – their name preceding the content of what is said or the first phrase repeated in case the children were not fully attending.

In listening to speech, a child will have to concentrate on the words and extract meaning from them. In the first part of the process, the child will be doing this with a minimum of or no visual information. We all use this kind of information in order to hear more clearly – we see a person's mouth moving, interpret a facial expression which adds meaning to the words, anticipate somebody joining in a conversation by noting a raised finger or an intake of breath. Without these clues, children will need to hear every word clearly and understand what is said solely with this verbal information. Concentrating may be easier

- in quiet surroundings;
- if the speaker allows time for information to be heard and absorbed (thus helping the child be relaxed);
- if there is variety in the speed, pitch and volume of the speaker's voice;
- if the child is engaged in the words through the use of frequent questions.

The adult can help, in ideal circumstances, by giving clear information and this was discussed in Chapter 5. Understanding what is said will also be easier if the child can develop techniques of active listening and this will be discussed later in this chapter.

Tape-recorders

Some children with visual impairment find they can use tape-recorded information very well. Others prefer the written word, even though it is slower to access. It is likely, though, that all children with visual impairment will need to use tape-recorded information, and particularly if they are studying in the later stages of secondary education or in higher education. For these children, using tape-recorders may, any way, be an important vocational skill.

Adults need to be able to understand and use the controls on tape-recorders and also to make good-quality recordings for children to use. What information and skills are needed to do this?

Some features on tape-recorders can be particularly helpful to listeners who are blind. Four-track recorders and variable speed help overcome two of the main disadvantages of tape recorders, the difficulty of searching through a tape for a specific section, and the slowness of listening to recordings of speech, much slower than silent reading of print.

Most tape-recorders use standard-size cassettes and record on each side of the cassette. When a recording is made, half the tape width is used and then, by turning over the tape, the other half of the tape is available to record a second track. However, in order to get more information on a tape, it is possible to obtain 4-track tape recorders. They work with standard cassettes but use one quarter of the tape each time a recording is made.

A second special feature which allows more information to be recorded on a tape is variable speed. Some tape-recorders – and most of those designed for use by people with visual impairment – allow the user to vary the speed at which the tape runs both during recording and playback. This enables the person making a recording to run the tape through the recorder very slowly, getting a lot of information on to the tape and it allows the listener to play back the recording at a higher speed and so be able to listen to the information as quickly as it is possible to understand it.

Both of these features can help with those difficulties mentioned above. Two additional features can be used in conjunction with the 4-track and variable-speed features. They are tone indexing and pitch correction. In order to help listeners to find their place on a tape, an indexing button will allow a tone, or series of tones, to be put on to the recording at appropriate places in the text. When the tape is being wound back or forward, the tones can be heard and so listeners are able to locate a specific section – perhaps the beginning of a chapter or section. A code of tones can be devised to identify various parts of a text. For example, chapter beginnings could be marked with five short tones and print pages indicated by two long tones. A more advanced technique is to use the index-ing facility on the second track of each side of the tape. If text is recorded on the first track, then the second, parallel, track can be used by the listener for notes and indexing. For example, as an important point in the text is reached, the recorder can be set to record on the second track and comments on the text added along with an indexing tone. This enables the listener to find that section of the text again easily, along with the com-ments on it. The second track acts a little like notes on a print text.

The second feature is the pitch-correction device and this is almost always used with the speeded-speech facility. As the tape is speeded up, the sound of the human voice is raised in pitch so that it produces a 'Mickey Mouse' effect. This is not easy to listen to nor, after a time, is it pleasant. In order to help intelligibility, the pitch-correction device adjusts the pitch of the voice into its natural register and this enables the listener to understand what is being said at speeds far in excess of those at which speech can be recorded. In fact, it is possible to understand speech at a speed of around 250 words per minute, roughly equivalent to a good silent-print-reading speed, although spoken speech is generally around 100 words per minute.

Making Recordings

Listening to tape-recordings can be difficult and tiring. A high-quality recording, though, will help considerably and it is necessary to give careful attention to the details of the recording technique in order to produce material which is pleasant, or even possible, to listen to over a long period of time. Making recordings requires consideration of five main areas. These are summarized below;

1 Arrange surroundings
   - location;
   - surface;
   - screening;
   - speaker.
2 Set up microphone
   - connections;
   - position.
3 Edit text
   - content;
   - visual material;
   - references glossary index;
   - markers;

- indexing.
4 Controls
  - track selector;
  - speed;
  - pause;
  - record.
5 Study notes

Arrange Surroundings

Recordings should be free from distracting background sounds and so the recording should be made in a place in which there will not be interference from sounds such as passing trains, people in a corridor, cars leaving a car park, extractor fan, telephone and so on. At certain times of the day a location may be much more free from possible interference than at other times and this should be considered in selecting a time for recording.

One common source of sound distraction is the table surface on which the recording is made. A cloth surface of carpet or even towelling is better than a noisy hard surface such as wood. The quality of sound can also be improved by using screens in front of the speaker. These not only help to cut out external sounds but also deaden echoes of the speaker's voice from the room, resulting in a sharper, clearer recording. The screens can be placed on the table and need to be at least as high as the speaker's head. They should be made of carpeting or other thick material which will absorb sound.

The speaker should, of course, have a pleasant voice but there is probably little preference in listeners for the voice of a man or woman. The speaker should be able to speak at a reasonably constant rate, particularly if the recording is to be used at an accelerated rate. Many inexperienced speakers increase their rate of talking as they go through a recording. It is most important that the speaker should understand the material that is being recorded and so can give an intelligible interpretation of the text with the correct and fluent pronunciation of any technical terms and names. If this is not the case, the listener is severely disadvantaged in having yet another burden to deal with.

Set up Microphone

Many cassette tape-recorders have built-in microphones and, while these can give adequate recordings, an external microphone is much more satisfactory. It may well be of higher quality and so make a clearer recording of the speech sounds and it can be located away from the tape-recorder motor and near the speaker. Most recorders have an external microphone socket into which this can be plugged.

Most microphones can pick up speech sounds best at 20–30 cm from the speaker's mouth. They should be positioned on a stand so that the speaker talks across the head of the microphone and not directly into it. This avoids the sound of the speaker appearing to be blowing into the microphone. Some microphones have a spongelike cover which will absorb these sounds.

Edit Text

This stage requires a good knowledge of the needs of the person who will be using the text. It may be that a straight reading of the printed text is required. Often, though, there is a need to identify passages that have to be altered because they draw on visual elements in the printed text, refer to other parts of the book which are not available or use concepts which the listener may not understand. A decision will often have to be made about how to present visual material such as graphs, tables, lists and pictures. Those showing relationships between elements (e.g. graphs) will be difficult to understand if described, and a tactile diagram will present the information much more satisfactorily. Some material will be included to add visual interest to the page and this can be easily identified and may be left out of the recording. Additional material, such as footnotes, can be made accessible if they are recorded straight after the relevant text. Finding passages on recordings can be much more difficult than with using print or braille. Glossaries, indexes and other lists of contents which may need to be referred to by the listener can be best recorded on a separate tape so that they are readily available when needed. Locating passages can also be easier if 'markers' are placed in the recording. These indicate when a page, paragraph or other section is started. It may, for example, be important for the listener to know which print page is being read. The 'markers' can simply be sentences recorded on the tape but they may be easier to identify when the tape is being wound on at speed (using the cue or review facility) if a tone, bleep or other sound precedes the marker. The tone can be made with an electronic bleeper, musical instrument or even humming or whistling. After a few seconds of that sound the speaker says the name of the page, chapter heading or other information that is needed. Some tape-recorders have an indexing facility which allows tones to be recorded on to the tape and this facility was mentioned earlier in this chapter.

Controls

Two decisions have to be made about the format of a recording. Firstly, with machines that have the possibility of 4-tracks, there is the choice of recording 2 or 4 tracks on a tape. Four tracks allow more material on the tape but, as the recording can only be played back on a 4-track machine, it is wise to record only 2 tracks if there is a possibility of the tape being used with a standard machine. Secondly, the speed at which the recording is made needs to be decided. Again, the standard speed should be used if it is likely that the tape will be played back on a one-speed recorder. Otherwise the slower speed will probably be the preferred option as it allows for more material on a tape, for a greater increase in speed of playback and quicker winding between sections of text.

Recordings should always be made by first pressing the pause control, then setting the recorder to record and finally starting the recorder using the pause control. The pause control should be used to stop and start the recorder as it is silent in operation. Using the stop and start controls will result in loud clicks on the tape which can be extremely distracting and irritating to the listener.

Study Notes
Listening demands a high level of concentration and students can be helped by being able to anticipate the structure and content of the text so that they can prepare themselves to listen to blocks of text and to listen actively through setting themselves questions to answer as they listen. This is part of the process of 'auding' discussed in the next section.

One way of helping listeners is to provide study notes which indicate the main section headings of chapters or give a summary of the author's main points. The content of these notes can be extracted from the text or may be part of the text. For example, chapter summaries, given at the end of chapters, are often skimmed through by print readers before they read the chapter in detail. The same information will be just as valuable to listeners but, as the section may not be as accessible, it could be recorded at the beginning of the taped chapter or provided in print or braille. Inexperienced listeners may be helped to develop their skill by quite detailed study notes which guide them through the text and suggest questions to which they should be listening for answers.

Skills for Children
If seeing is equivalent to hearing and looking equivalent to listening, then the term 'auding' (coined by Trowald 1975) is equivalent to reading. It involves listening for meaning and so being actively involved in the content of the text. Auding involves being able to maintain concentration and to extract information. With tape-recordings it may also involve coping with speed listening. Listening skills may not, therefore, be an accurate term to describe what we are concerned with here. We want children to learn to listen but also to 'aud' – interpret and understand the sounds.

Bishop (1971) has suggested a number of exercises which can help children develop these skills and these are particularly useful for preparing children to use tape-recordings. For example, she suggests that when listening a child might be encouraged to;

Listen for *factual details*. This may be practised through setting questions about facts in the passage which the child should listen for.

Use *selective listening*. Activities can be given to a child, or groups of children in which they have to pick out certain sounds from amongst other distracting background noises or identify out-of-place phrases in a passage.

Develop *informative listening*. This requires a child to identify the main, or topic, sentence in a passage.

Use *evaluative listening*. The child should identify if opinions or facts are being expressed and may go on to separate statements from supporting evidence.

Bishop's book, although written some time ago, contains many suggestions which are still of help today. Other detailed suggestions for listening can be found in Stocker (1973); Bischoff (1979) provides a good summary and bibliography; the Open University produce a very informative document entitled 'Notes for visually handicapped students'.

Children also need to be able to use a tape-recorder. Listening is usually more comfortable and easy if it is through headphones and so this should be encouraged. The standard controls may be familiar, but many children will need help with adjusting the speed control, track selector and indexing facility. In each case, children will need practice in using the actual control and in understanding when to use each facility.

The speed control (usually with pitch correction) is simple to operate but good understanding of speeded speech at the most efficient speed will require a series of exercises. The most efficient speed will be the fastest at which the child can achieve full comprehension. This will vary for different types of materials. A high speed is likely to be achieved when listening to familiar material or text that is easy for the child to understand. A slower speed will be needed for complex passages, those containing a number of critical points or at times when, for one reason of another, the child is having difficulty concentrating. The child, then, must be confident in adjusting speed to suit the material and feel able to wind back over a passage if necessary.

Achieving the maximum speed may involve the teacher giving some practice sessions in listening. One approach is to encourage the child to listen for only the main points in a passage, while setting the speed rather higher than is comfortable. With practice, the child should be able to gain confidence through success and so the 'threshold' of speed can be increased. This approach is similar to that used in speed reading.

Operating the track control is simple but its use, in combination with indexing to add notes to a tape, presents a challenge that is likely to restrict its use to older secondary-age children. It is at this stage of education when the process of making notes on text, perhaps in preparation for compiling information in an essay, is likely to be of importance. There are no training materials available to develop these skills, but a teacher can devise a series of exercises using text relevant to a particular child which will take the child through each of the sub-skills needed. This will include practice at the following sequence:

- Stopping the tape with the pause button.
- Pressing the stop button.
- Changing tracks with the track-selection switch.
- Putting the recorder into record mode.
- Starting the tape with the pause button.

The child will then need to devise and record an indexing code to indicate the type of information that is to be recorded (e.g. section heading; summary; comments; references). Compiling the note is also a skill but one that is also needed when using print or braille.

To use the information the child will need to be able to retrieve it easily. The sequence that should lead to this skill involves practice at:

- Winding the tape forward and backwards;
- Pressing the pause and stop buttons as soon as the appropriate tone is heard;
- Pressing the play and then pause buttons to listen to the note;
- Switching tracks to hear the original text;
- Using cue and review to locate passages and re-listen to a section.

Summary

The use of listening is likely to be important for children with visual impairments, both to help them understand what is happening around them, and to gain information which might otherwise be accessible through print. Teachers and children need to be familiar with tape-recorders so that they can be used easily as part of the everyday equipment, allowing children access to print material.

CHAPTER 10

Movement and Mobility

In Chapter 1 several examples were given of the kind of situations in which a child with visual impairments may have difficulty in movement – understanding what a straight line is; locating and interpreting sounds; getting direct access to the surroundings, such as road surfaces, to find out what they are like. In this chapter we will examine movement, orientation and mobility. Each of these have a slightly different meaning. The term 'motor development' covers many, but not all, of the skills with which we are concerned. Orientation is the ability to understand surroundings through an awareness of space and spatial relationships between objects and people in the environment. Mobility is the ability to travel through the surroundings and the term 'movement' is used here to describe the motor skills needed in order to reach, crawl, walk or run. The ability to walk round a classroom or, more challengingly, through open space such as a playground, requires a combination of skills. Certainly motor skills are required. But a child will also need a certain level of cognitive skill to remember the route and understand what is happening. Motivation, including confidence, will be needed. Language skills will be required to understand directions. The coordinated use of several senses – touch, vision, hearing, kinesthetic – will enable the child to monitor direction and space. The following list gives the areas covered in the Peabody Mobility Scale (Harley *et al*. 1981) and shows the range of skills that can be considered part of this area.

- Motor Development
  - basic movement;

- crawling;
- standing;
- walking;
- ascending stairs;
- descending stairs;
- running;
- jumping;
- climbing.
- Sensory skills
  - Sound localization;
  - tactual discrimination (hands);
  - tactual discrimination (feet);
  - olfactory discrimination.
- Concept development
  - body image;
  - spatial relations (front/back; up/down; on/under);
  - left–right discrimination;
  - shape discrimination;
  - size discrimination;
  - organization.
- Mobility skills
  - Sighted guide;
  - seating;
  - turning and maintaining orientation;
  - trailing;
  - utilization of discriminate landmarks;
  - environmental travel.

Specialist training is available for staff wanting to acquire in-depth understanding of this area. But all staff should feel some responsibility for the development of these skills as they are used in all aspects of daily living. As early development has been shown to be crucial in the acquisition of skills later, those with the child during the pre-school years are also likely to be involved in helping the development of effective mobility. Mobility is needed by the child at all times and there are many opportunities to help and encourage a child to build up a mental map of the surrounding spaces and develop strategies to move accurately and safely through them.

Problem Areas

A number of writers have described possible difficulties that visually handicapped children might experience in motor development and have suggested solutions. For example Cratty and Sams (1968) developed a scale for the assessment of critical skills; Fraiberg (1977) describes a number of case studies of blind children who learn motor skills; Reynell (1978) examined the pattern of motor development in a number of young visually handicapped children; Murphy and O'Driscoll (1989) summarize many of the difficulties and suggest how physiotherapists might help; Warren (1984) has a detailed summary of all major research publications in this area up to that date. Sonksen *et al.* (1984) has suggested seven ways in which the motor development of blind children may be constrained. This forms an excellent summary of the problems that need solving and can provide a structure for our examination of this area.

Diminished Drive

Sonksen defines this as 'that quality of personality that urges exploration, participation and mastery' (p. 274). Lack of vision will take away one important reason children have for moving about – to get to something interesting. Particularly for boys, a reason for moving is to take risks, perhaps by jumping off the swing or diving for a ball. At school, the reason for moving for a child with visual impairments may be very functional – simply to get to the next lesson. This may be his primary motivation and reason for learning, unlike the other children who think of moving in terms of skills at games and recreation. The absence of this drive can be observed in the first few months of life when there is, typically, a delay in the onset of reaching and crawling in the visually handicapped infant.

Poor Body Image

Body image involves realizing the potential functional capacity of different parts of the body. Lack of vision may result in lack of knowledge of what the body can do – how it can bend, stretch and move. It is difficult to sit up straight if you have never seen anybody else sit up straight; marching 'like a soldier' is difficult if you have never felt, or seen, a soldier marching. Many physical-education activities and games can help children develop an accurate body image. A child and adult can move together, making their bodies perform similar or reflective movements; children can be asked to make their bodies into different shapes – a ball, a long thin shape or a stiff shape; children can work together making each other's bodies into different shapes.

Reduced Opportunity

Lack of vision reduces the opportunities there are to develop and use movement skills. The author recalls a 15-year-old blind girl who said that her main regret was not being able to fool around with her friends in the evening. Maybe they would throw a can into a litter bin or dash across the road between cars. She felt her lack of vision prevented her from joining in, both because of her lack of ability and their lack of willingness to be held back by her clumsiness. Adults may reduce the opportunities available to a blind child in order to protect them from a potentially dangerous situation. Sonsken, for example, identifies a father's reluctance to engage in rough-and-tumble play with a blind child. The children may not attempt some movements because their lack of ability to imitate prevents them from realizing that the movement is possible. Very often this constraint can be helped by adults – parents and teachers – creating opportunities. At school and home the child can collect equipment, carry messages, play freely in the garden and be given help in complex skills like bicycle riding.

Delay in Formation of Basic Concepts

Particularly up to the age of 8, moving around requires an understanding of concepts such as in front of, behind, here, above. These are all positional concepts. Children also need to understand comparative concepts such as nearer and further. Children cannot walk to somebody in front of them unless they realize there is an 'out there' and understand what 'in front of' means in any specific situation. For several reasons – including lack of motivation and lack of experience at perceiving spatial relations – children with visual impairments are likely to be delayed in acquiring a concept of permanence of objects and in the formation of the subsequent basic concepts. Practice can be given to help development and this may include activities involving collecting and placing objects around the child; the children describing where they are in relation to an object or person; building models using blocks of Lego to a pattern described by an adult.

Sensori-motor Integration

Many movements we make successfully are the result of several senses working together. If we reach for a cup, then our hand movement is adjusted by the information our eyes are giving us about the position of the hand in relation to the cup. The integration of a sensory input – in this case vision – with motor responses allows us to perform the action.

For blind children, one particular difficulty is adjusting to changes in position. We see from eye-height outwards and, at a glance, can see the view in front of us. When we change position, say by moving round a room, we have little difficulty in understanding the room from our new viewpoint. Blind children cannot do this as they do not have that fixed point of view and for them a change in position may result in difficulties. This starts at a very early stage when the infant is beginning to realize that the floor is a solid base to the world – that it is he that moves, not the floor. Practice will be needed at moving between objects almost within reach to help build images of spaces, distances, directions based on information from movement, sounds and touch. This could be provided by moving between a sofa and a chair and table and then moving from the chair and reaching for the sofa and table. Later tactile plans of rooms can be used to imagine where objects would be when standing in various places in the room.

A second difficulty can be in sound localization. This is no substitute for visually directed reaching in the first few months of life and yet will be a valuable skill in mobility. The use of hearing to direct movement can be practised throughout pre-school, primary and secondary schooling. It will begin as the concept of permanence of objects develops through activities such as reaching for a musical box in front of the child. Much later, children will develop more sophisticated skills such as calculating direction through games of chasing and finding.

Fear

The seventh of Sonksen's constraints results from lack of familiarity with situations and from attitudes of others to the child's attempts at movement. It may be overcome through acquiring familiarity (repetition and practice); through the acquisition of skills; and through the confidence that can come from realistically high expectations.

Early Movement

The development of early movement in children with visual impairments typically shows variations from normal development. The ages at which milestones are reached are often delayed, the gaps between the acquisition of skills may appear abnormal but, more significantly, the order in which some skills develop seems to be different. For example, a child will often start shuffling backwards before forwards and may begin to walk before crawling on hands and knees. Most significantly for encouraging development, the experiences which result in the acquisition of new skills may be different. For example a child is unlikely to develop head control through trying to look into a mirror, a common activity to help sighted children. Instead the child may need to be physically guided through head movements and be rewarded for making appropriate movements with a favourite sound or verbal praise.

The development of early movements was described in Chapter 7, 'Tactile Skills', within a framework of zones (face, body, personal, social and group) and this concept and the associated activities can form a basis for movement work, particularly for multi-handicapped children. The use of each hand and then the co-ordinated use of both hands will be important first stages in developing body movements and body awareness. These may be movements on the body resulting in body sounds: with the hands, on objects that make a sound (e.g. bells, greaseproof paper, plastic plates); with the hands moving against materials with a texture (e.g. artificial grass, bead curtains, velvet clothing); with the hands holding objects which can make a sound when banged. In each case, movements result in a sound or tactile reward. One important lesson that is being learnt is that of cause and effect. A body movement results in something's happening, such as a sound, as well as a physical feeling. There is an 'out-there' which can provide stimulation and can be responsive. For the child, touching something or making a movement produces a reward. Some activities can use sophisticated equipment. For example, a tape-recorder activated by an infra-red light-beam switch. When the child raises a hand, it would break the light beam and set the tape-recorder playing for a few seconds. Other activities could be simpler, as when an adult blows on the child's face every time both hands are brought together.

After this stage, whole body movements can be encouraged. Development of crawling, standing and walking involve motor and orientation skills. The outline from the Peabody Scale given above shows the kind of related sensory and cognitive skills that might parallel this development. An alternative developmental sequence is given in the Oregon Project (Brown *et al*. 1991) listed under the heading 'Gross motor skills'. Both of these materials include many suggestions for training activities to accompany each developmental stage.

McInnes and Treffry (1982) suggest that activities at this stage may be seen as co-active, co-operative or reactive. In co-active activities the adult and child act as one person with the child being given a great deal of physical prompting. At the co-operative stage, the adult provides the child with sufficient support and guidance to ensure success. At the reactive stage, the child completes the activity independently. The child has now learnt to imitate the action of the adult through being given appropriate experiences.

These are not just stages, though, as the authors suggest they should be seen in terms of a total reactive environment in which interactions allow the child to learn rather than being directive in nature. They define a reactive environment as one characterized by:

Emotional bonding and, as the child grows and develops, social respon-
siveness.
Problem-solving to reinforce the development of a positive self-image.
Utilization of residual vision and hearing and the integration of input with
that from other sensory modalities.
Communication, with an emphasis on dialogue.

(McInnes and Treffry 1982: 28)

This concept, of course, covers the whole process of learning and not just motor development but fits in particularly well with motor-based activities as the authors' detailed chapter on motor development illustrates.

The Reynell-Zinkin scales includes a sub-scale on Room Orientation which examines children's ability to find their way around furniture and across rooms. This can be valuable in alerting an adult to this special developmental area which is left out of most other developmental scales. A number of related research studies have recently examined this area of pre-school orientation and mobility (Best 1985; Culpan 1988; Furth 1989). Their work has resulted in a pilot assessment scale with training activities in the areas of Posture and Gait, Gross Motor Development, Body Awareness, Room Orientation. These four areas seem to represent discrete and relevant skills areas at this developmental stage.

Posture includes skills in sitting, standing and walking, such as holding the head upright, sitting with straight back, swinging the arms when walking. Children may need to be corrected to develop good habits in these areas. The child who is congenitally blind will have no model of good posture to copy and so is sure to need help in developing good posture. This may be through being reminded, through touching other people to understand what is required, using dolls to demonstrate positions and movements, through specific exercises such as those described by Tooze (1981). The child who is adventitiously blind may have some visual memories which can be recalled to help particularly during teenage years when the young person may be most motivated to develop good posture. Some children with very poor vision, although able to use this to gain some impression of other people's posture and gait, will have a severe problem in needing to adopt unusual postures in order to use their vision most effectively – perhaps bending over a table to get close to an object or holding the head on one side to use a narrow field of vision. There is no simple answer to this situation but unusual postures are likely to be ergonomically unsound and put stress on the body, so they need to be avoided if possible. The adult can check that the child is making efficient use of any vision, as outlined in Chapter 8; the use of aids and adaptations can then be considered, for example, in altering the angle of a table surface or the height of a chair; training in the use of a distance-vision aid. Chapter 6 gives more information about these. Next, the need for an unusual posture may have to be accepted and for this the adult can help the child identify the situations in which it is necessary.

The second area of gross motor development covers skills such as walking forwards and backwards, walking over different surfaces, climbing stairs, balancing on one leg, kicking a ball. The points identified by Sonksen above and by McInnes and Treffry are all pertinent to this area, as are activities suggested by the latter and by Tooze.

Body awareness in this context is concerned with children's knowledge of parts of their body, the relationships between them, and their potential for movement. This involves naming parts of the body, orientating the body into specified positions, recognizing parts of other peoples' bodies. Finger-play games and rhymes about parts of the body can help a child develop this understanding. Adults can make a point of talking about movements and positions, while allowing a child to touch their body and feel it moving. Children can play games with a partner – making themselves and their partner into shapes such as long, round, small; walking round their partner with one shoulder touching all the time; stepping, jumping and rolling over a partner lying on the floor. Activities such as these may help a child, at the appropriate developmental stage, to understand movements their body can make but may also help in creating an understanding of the space around the body and the person's position in that space. One checklist that concentrates on this specific area is the Test of Positional Concepts (Hill 1984). This lists a wide range of locational (e.g. in front of, above) and comparative (e.g. nearer, further away) concepts. The list can be used to check through a child's understanding of these concepts and so identify any concept that needs developing.

The fourth area is room orientation. This involves a child finding his way between parts of a room and between rooms. An assessment checklist can be devised for a specific building with routes within and between areas listed. Then the child can be observed negotiating these routes. It is sometimes helpful for assessment to divide up a route into component sub-routes so that more precise recording can be made of a child's performance. Another exercise which can help an adult identify the child's performance is to record exactly where a child travels within an area. This may be particularly helpful for use with very young or multi-handicapped children. A plan of the area can be made and then the child's movements plotted over a period of time. From this information, an impression can be built up of the clues and landmarks the child may be using. The child's concept of the area may be deduced by identifying the parts of the area which are most travelled over and those that are never entered.

To help a child develop skills in room orientation and travel, routes can be divided up into small segments and the available clues identified. Children can then be given practice in finding their way over these small segments and their attention drawn to the clues that may help them. Children may need practice at finding their way to a particular part of a room from different places so that they can build up a mental map of the space that makes up the room. They will also need to learn routes one direction at a time, as the clues may be quite different when travelling in opposite directions. This approach is discussed in some detail by Best (1987a) in relation to people with severe learning difficulties.

Gradually the routes can be increased in length and complexity and this moves the activity into more formal mobility which is discussed in the next section of this chapter.

Routes can be practised as part of mobility sessions, but there are also many opportunities for practice during the rest of the day. Children can be asked to fetch things, expected to put away their toys and equipment, take messages and help with tidying up around the house and classroom. In this respect every adult can think of himself as a teacher of mobility and every activity as part of mobility training. This is, probably, particularly important at this early stage when expectations of the child may be as critical as skills teaching in determining success.

Formal Mobility

Children will use a combination of information from different senses to help them travel independently. Information from aromas can help in identifying and locating rooms, shops and people. Changes in temperature can indicate the presence of an object (for example, a tree, wall or building) which cuts off the sun from the traveller's face. The kinesthetic sense provides information about muscle movements. It is this sense which helps us to know that we are walking uphill or along a slope. In the absence of reliable visual information, this sense will help a child monitor body movements and may help particularly in travelling in a straight line. The sense of touch is a major source of information and provides *foot* clues and *hand* clues. *Sound* clues, mentioned in Chapter 9, can be another major source of information and have the advantage of providing information at a distance. Remaining vision, when present, is likely to be invaluable, although it may well need to be used in combination with other information. These major types of information will each be discussed.

Fig 10.1 (a) and (b)   Mobility training gives a child techniques to move safely and confidently.
Photo: B. Dallimore, RNIB New College, Worcester.

Hand Clues

Hand clues are any pieces of information that are obtained through the hands. They can usually be discerned through 'trailing' – the hand is held in front of and to the side of the body with the back of the hand forwards. In this way the fingers are not forced backwards if they unexpectedly hit an object. Children can be alerted to many naturally occurring hand clues. Banisters are an example. They are most helpful if they are continuous and finish at least level with the bottom step so that the end of the banisters clearly indicates the end of the steps. Door handles, dado rails, table surfaces, wall coverings and so on can all be used to help establish position and direction of movement. Hand clues can also be introduced into a setting to provide extra support for a child. Plastic or wooden shapes can be fastened on to a child's chair, drawer and peg to make them

Figure 10.1 (b)

easier to find; textured wallpaper can be added to a wall just in front of a door or near the beginning of a flight of stairs; distinctive handles can be used to help in the identification of different doors in a corridor. These extra clues need not necessarily draw attention to the blind child's special needs. For example, warning of a door in a corridor could be given by gluing several strands of nylon fishing line to the wall to form a tactile patch of vertical stripes. It will be easily felt by the child but go unnoticed by many sighted people.

Foot Clues

Information available directly through the feet is often about edges between surfaces – the path and grass, carpet and lino, pavement and road. The texture of a surface can also be of help and Chapter 4 discussed some ways in which these clues can be built into an environment. The 'white stick' can also be used with this type of information. In fact the term 'white stick' is rarely used now and the correct name for the well-known mobility aid is 'long cane'. This is a specially constructed stick of aluminium tubing which needs to be carefully matched to the height of the user. The tip is moved with a sweeping action in front of the user, giving warning of any obstacles and information about the surface. Techniques of use enable a user to negotiate any common hazard including stairs, holes in the road, even revolving doors, while the regular information gathered with every sweep helps with orientation. Mobility officers can teach children the many skills required to use a long cane. Although teachers of the visually handicapped are usually trained in mobility, their training stops short of the specialist skills required to teach long-cane use.

The long cane is intended particularly for use in unfamiliar locations. In familiar settings, such as a home or school, a child may well be able to use foot, hand and sound clues to achieve efficient mobility and need not be

Figure 10.2 This corridor has four floor surfaces which are different both tactually and visually.

encumbered by a cane. The age at which a child should start training in long-cane use is a matter for debate. It requires motor skills to handle the cane movement, motivation to move in unfamiliar surroundings and maturity to be able to travel alone in streets. Often children are introduced to some of the techniques of use at around the age of 7 with more intensive training being given from the age of 11.

Sound Clues

Under this heading come the skills of identification, location and use of echoes and sound shadows. The use of sounds for mobility was mentioned in the previous chapter on listening skills. The interested reader will find valuable additional information in Welsh and Blasch (1980) and Dodds (1988).

To help develop skills in identifying sounds, adults can talk to children and comment on why sounds have occurred and what has made them. Children can be asked questions about sounds and asked to interpret what they think is making a sound or what they think is happening. It can be very helpful for children to be able to make the sounds themselves so that they have first-hand experience of how the sounds are made. This skill can be used to build up an awareness of what is happening in any situation. This may alert the child to potential hazards or help in identifying people or activities that the child might want to join.

Sound location is a vital skill in orientation and mobility and involves locating both stationary and moving sounds. A child will need to locate the position of stationary sounds in order to plan routes through an area. Preliminary practice in this skill can be given through games such as finding sound-making toys – a clock or musical box can be placed at a distance from the child who has to locate it. The toy can be placed at different heights as well as various directions from the child. Memory for sound location can be practised through having a child find a toy after it has made a sound for a few seconds.

The next stage is probably for the child to follow a moving sound. This can be the adult moving around making a sound such as clicking the fingers or clapping. The child can chase and try to catch the adult. A more difficult variation would be for the child to have to grasp a sound-making toy that the adult is holding rather than just locate the adult. For this activity, not only direction needs to be established quite precisely but also distance. This seems to be considerably more difficult to judge, perhaps because using both ears and head movements enables direction to be perceived through comparing the input from each side, while judgements about distance will depend on less exact and consistent information about volume of sounds.

Next the child will need to be able to judge speed, direction and distance of moving objects. This skill will be needed for safe travel. Though it can be practised as a group activity with a class of children, individual sessions may also be needed so that a child can be taken, for example, to a roadside to learn to make judgements about when it is safe to cross a road. A final stage is to locate the direction of moving sounds when the child is also moving. This is an extension of the chasing game described above but the aim is now to negotiate around the object, not just get closer to it.

The use of sound shadows and echoes enables a child to locate objects, and potential hazards. Areas of sound shadow are created when a solid object comes between a sound source and the child. An example of this would be a door which, when closed, alters the quality of sound coming from a room. A bus shelter can be located by the sound shadow it creates as it masks the sound of traffic. A child walking along the side of a building may locate the end of the wall by noticing the change in sounds coming from behind the building. Echoes are used, sometimes unknowingly, to judge distance and location of objects. Experienced blind travellers sometimes make sounds by clicking the fingers or tapping a foot, from which they can determine the presence of objects. This can lead to establishing the size of a room, the proximity of a door or even the location of very difficult objects like post boxes and lampposts. At one time it was thought that some blind people possessed 'facial vision', an extra sense which enabled them to be aware of objects near to them. This was sometimes described by blind people as like feeling the presence of the object through pressure on the face. Experiments in the 1960s examined this phenomenon and found that, if the blind person's hearing was taken away through the use of ear plugs, they were no longer able to make successful judgements. It seemed that, without realizing it, they were using sound echoes from noises they made, environmental sounds or even the sound of their breathing. With practice some children can develop this skill. They can listen in quiet rooms to guess when a large piece of card is moved in front of their face; they can try to guess which of two walls is nearer to them; they can judge when a door in front of them is open or closed. Gradually the distances can be increased and the size of the target object reduced, until the skill becomes generalized to use in mobility routes.

Residual Vision

The assessment of distance vision for use in mobility was discussed in Chapter 8. In particular, the need to examine a child's performance in both familiar and unfamiliar situations was emphasized. Further details about this topic can be found in Welsh and Blasch (1980) and Jose (1983).

Figure 10.3   The handle and sign stand out visually and can also be easily identified tactually.

The visual skills needed for mobility may well parallel those identified as being needed in near vision. The ability to scan and search and to recognize critical features seems likely to be of particular importance. The type of visual defect will have an influence on the use of these skills as the visual ambiguities created by specific defects will be different. Systematic scan-and-search skills may be particularly important for children who have an interrupted or narrow field of vision. Beck (1988) has suggested a sequence of skills needed by people using monocular telescopes for distance viewing and this can provide one framework for developing scan and search techniques. The skills area:

- localize objects;
- focus on moving object at constant distance;
- follow object moving towards and away;

- follow object requiring both focusing and tracking as above, but while moving.

The recognition of critical features requires an understanding of object constancy in order to recognize an object from different points of view. This should develop in children in the first few years of life, although some children with visual impairments will need extra practice in the primary-school years to acquire this concept in relation to common distant objects. The critical features that are most helpful in many mobility situations will be edges. The edge between stairs and a wall, for example, will show up the size and length of the flight of stairs; the edge between a wall and floor will help in identifying the shape and size of a room; the edge between the back of a chair and the background wall may help to locate the position of one object in front of another. Shadows can sometimes be helpful in creating a clear visual edge to a step but features that are available in the morning may disappear in the afternoon sun. Another method of identifying foreground/background differences is for children to move their head while looking, so that the relative position of objects becomes apparent.

Figure 10.4 Specially designed paths with varying surfaces and a clear edge. *Photo: B. Dallimore, RNIB New College, Worcester.*

Multi-handicapped Children

The needs of children with severe learning difficulties were discussed in the section on early movement. If these children reach the stage of attempting independent travel, then all the points made above will be relevant. What they may need is extra help in building up confidence to move, particularly if the child has had many unsuccessful experiences in the past. Routes may need to be broken down into very small stages, with a child expected to attempt only a few steps at a time. The teaching approach of task analysis, which is commonly used for teaching many skills to children with learning difficulties, will be very appropriate for this type of activity. The amount of support, or prompting, will also need to be carefully controlled. Take, for example, a boy who is severely visually handicapped and with severe learning difficulties, who walks unsteadily and resists attempts to have him walk over grass. The activity can be broken into a developmental sequence of touching the grass, sitting on it, crawling on it, standing on it, walking with support, walking independently. As the child progresses from standing to moving, the adult can help the child by standing in front of him holding both his hands and pulling him just a step or two towards the adult. Gradually the distance can be increased with the adult walking backwards, still holding on to the child's hands. The hand grip can then be changed so that the adult is holding the child's wrists and is able to leave go of the child for a few seconds. If the child knows he is walking towards something appealing – a piece of fruit, drink, tickle, toy – then this will make the activity more likely to be successful than if the exercise is simply a mobility activity. The adult can gradually reduce the amount of support that is given by walking behind the child, holding on to his waist or shoulder so that the child has his hands free to discover hand clues if they are available.

Summary

The area of movement and mobility is an important part of the special curriculum for children with visual impairments. From early movement through to independent travel, the child may need extra help to overcome the constraints imposed by visual limitations. Touch, hearing and vision can all be used by the child to provide valuable information to orientate themselves in their environment and will also give access to clues that can enable safe travel through the environment.

Postscript

Perhaps, on reflection, every decade seems to have contained major changes in education. The 1980s have certainly seen great changes in our field of visual impairment. The type of child needing services has changed, so that now probably over 70 per cent have very significant additional handicaps. The figure at the beginning of the decade was probably around 20 per cent. The pattern of placements has changed profoundly with less than 50 per cent of children now attending special schools. In 1980, over 90 per cent of the children attended special schools. Technology has enabled us to produce braille materials quickly and given children direct access to print materials. From one teacher-training course of 12 places in 1980, we now have 5 centres with 145 places in 1990.

More general trends in education have affected our field. For example, the involvement of parents in educational decision-making has resulted in closer collaboration between professionals and parents in planning and in teaching. The development of a National Curriculum has affected all schools and pupils but, in particular, is having a major effect on children with visual impairments who need a supplementary curriculum and whose learning problems result in them being unable to achieve some SAT targets at the same time as other children. The development of Local Management of Schools and of Special Schools may well effect the availability of support services for children integrated into mainstream schools.

Many of these developments are taking place as we move into the 1990s and it will be several years before we shall be clear about the way ahead and have resolved the current uncertainties. Some parts of this book will be made obsolete by advances in technology, legislation or educational practice. It is unlikely, though, that any medical development will over-come the visual defects which result in partial sight or blindness. The children will still be with us. They will still need informed adults – as parents or professionals – to understand them and to have the skills to help them learn and develop. Technology will not remove that need for knowledge and skills.

I hope that this book has contained some useful information for those of you engaged in this work. If so, then the children will be the better for it. That aim is probably what unites us all in our efforts, whether we are here through circumstance or choice. I am reminded of a blind friend who was asked whether he preferred a guide dog or long cane to help his mobility. 'Neither,' he replied, 'I use bumps and bruises.' That confidence and spirit had come through having the opportunity to develop, through access to vital experiences and through skilled teaching. He had been accepted as an individual and had developed as an individual. I hope this book has provided a framework of principles and information which will allow us to help children to develop in their own way and enable them to be the individuals they can be.

References

Atkinson, J. and Braddick, O. (1979). 'New techniques for assessing vision in infants and young children', *Child Care, Health and Development* 389–98.

Backman, O. and Inde, K. (1982). *Low Vision Training*. Sweden, Liber Hemods.

Barraga, N.C. and Morris, J.E. (1989). *Program to Develop Efficiency in Visual Functioning*. Louisville, Kentucky, American Printing House for the Blind.

Beck, B. (1988). 'Low vision mobility'. In N. Neustadt-Noy *et al*. (eds), *Orientation and Mobility for the Visually Handicapped*. Jerusalem, Heiliger.

Bell, J. (1983). 'The stimulation of visual attention in the profoundly multi-handicapped child'. University of Birmingham, B. Phil. dissertation.

Bell, J. (1986). 'The profoundly handicapped, visually handicapped child', *British Journal of Visual Impairment* 4(2): 46–8.

Benton, S. (1982). *Supporting Visually Handicapped Children in Ordinary Schools*. University of Birmingham, unpublished dissertation.

Bentzen, B.L. and Peck, A.F. (1979). 'Factors affecting traceability of lines for tactile graphics', *Journal of Visual Impairment and Blindness* 73: 243–89.

Best, A.B. (1986). 'Approaches to teaching people with visual and mental handicaps'. In D. Ellis (ed.), *Sensory Impairments in Mentally Handicapped People*. London, Croom Helm.

Best, A.B. (1987a). *Steps to Independence*. Kidderminster, British Institute of Mental Handicap.

Best, A.B. (1987b). 'Assessment procedures for use with young visually handicapped children' (Part 1), *British Journal of Visual Impairment* V(3): 85–8.

Best, A.B. *et al*. (1987). *Out of Isolation*. London, Royal National Institute for the Blind.

Best, A.B. (1988). 'Assessment of procedures for use with young visually handicapped children' (Part II), *British Journal of Visual Impairment* VI(1): 7–10.

Best, C. (1983). 'The new deaf-blind', *British Journal of Visual Impairment* **1**(2): 11–13.

Best, C. (1985). 'Educational psychologists and visually impaired children: current practice and future development'. University of Birmingham, M. Ed. thesis.

Bischoff, R.W. (1979). 'Listening – a teachable skill', *Journal of Visual Impairment and Blindness* **73**(2): 59–65.

Bishop, V.E. (1971). *Teaching the Visually Limited Child*. Springfield, Charles Thomas.

Bishop, V.E. (1986). 'Identifying components of success in mainstreaming', *Journal of Visual Impairment and Blindness* **80**(9): 939–46.

Boyce, P. (1981). *Human Factors in Lighting*. London, Academic Press.

Brown, D. *et al.* (1991). *Oregon Project*. Medford, Oregon, Jackson County Education District, revised edition.

Buell, C.E. (1982). *Physical Education and Recreation for the Visually Handicapped*. Reston, Va., American Alliance for Health.

Buell, C.E. (1983). *Physical Education for Blind Children*. Springfield, Ill., Charles C. Thomas.

Chapman, E.K. and Stone, J.M. (1988). *The Visually Handicapped Child in Your Classroom*. London, Cassell.

Clamp, S.A. (1988). 'An investigation into the mathematical understanding of number operations'. University of Birmingham, M. Ed. thesis.

Colborne-Brown, M.A. and Tobin, M.S. (1982). 'Integration of the educationally blind', *New Beacon* **LXVI** (781): 113–17.

Corn, A.L. (1983). 'Visual function: a theoretical model for individuals with low vision', *Journal of Visual Impairment and Blindness* **77**(9): 373–7.

Cratty, B.J. and Sams, T.A. (1968). *The Body Image of Blind Children*. New York, American Foundation for the Blind.

Cullinan, T.R. (1977). *The Epidemiology of Visual Disability*. University of Kent Health Services Research Unit.

Culpan, J. (1988). 'A pilot evaluation of some criterion-referenced orientation and mobility checklists for use with pre-school visually impaired children'. University of Birmingham, M. Ed. thesis.

Dawkins, J. (1990). *Bright Horizons*. London, Royal National Institute for the Blind.

Department of Education and Science (1985). *Design Note 25; Designing Classrooms for Pupils with a Visual Impairment*. London, HMSO.

Diderot, M. (1845) [1773]. *Essay on Blindness*. London, Sampson Low.

Dobree, J.H. and Boulter, E. (1982). *Blindness and Visual Handicap: The Facts*. Oxford, Oxford University Press.

Dodds, A. (1988). *Mobility Training for Visually Handicapped People*. London, Croom Helm.

Elks, D. (1986). 'The epidemiology of visual impairment in people with a mental handicap'. In D. Ellis (ed.), *Sensory Handicaps in the Mentally Handicapped*. London, Croom Helm.

Ellis, D. (ed.) (1986). *Sensory Impairments in Mentally Handicapped People*. London, Croom Helm.

Ferrell, K.A. (1980). *Reach Out and Teach*. New York, American Foundation for the Blind.

Fitt, R.A. and Mason, H. (1986). *Sensory Handicaps in Children*. Stratford-on-Avon, National Council for Special Education.

Fletcher, R.C. (ed.) (1970). *Teaching Science and Mathematics to the Blind*. London, Royal National Institute for the Blind.

Ford, M. (1986). *In Touch*. London, BBC Publications.

Fothergill, S.C. (1980). 'Turn over the page – a history of St Vincent's School, Liverpool'. University of Birmingham, B. Phil. (ed.) dissertation.

Fraiberg, S. (1977). *Insights From the Blind*. London, Souvenir Press.

Fullwood, D. (1984). *A Start to Independence for Young Visually Handicapped Child*. Melbourne, Royal Victorian Institute for the Blind.

Furth, A.T. (1989). 'An evaluation of sections of a pre-school mobility checklist and a collection of activities to be used with the checklist'. University of Birmingham, B. Phil. (ed.) dissertation.

Griffiths, M.I. (1979). 'Associated disorders in children with severe handicaps'. In V. Smith and J. Keen (eds), *Visual Handicap in Children*. London, Heinemann.

Guillie, S. (1918). *The Instruction and Amusements of the Blind*. Paris, Academy for the Blind.

Harley, R.K. *et al*. (1981). *Peabody Mobility Kit*. Chicago, Stoelting.

Harris, L.J. (1980). 'Which hand is the "eye" of the blind'. In J. Herron (ed.), *Neuropsychology of Left-handedness*. San Diego, Calif., Academic Press.

Heritage, R.S. (1986). *A Guide to the Teaching of Maths at the Primary Level to Pupils with Visual Handicaps*. Research Centre for Education of the Visually Handicapped, University of Birmingham.

Hermelin, B. and O'Connor, N. (1971). 'Functional asymmetry in the reading of braille', *Neuropsychology* 9: 431–5.

Hill, E.E. (1984). *Test of Positional Concepts*. Chicago, Stoelting.

Hinton, R. (1988). *New Ways With Diagrams*. London, Royal National Institute for the Blind.

Holly, V. (1786). *An Essay on the Education of the Blind*. Paris, Academy for the Blind.

Hyvarinen, L. (1983). *Assessment of Vision in Children*. Fack, Sweden, Tomteboda School.

Hyvarinen, L. (1985). 'Classification of visual impairment and disability', *Bulletin Sociétié belge Ophthalmologie* 215: 1–16.

Hyvarinen, L. (1988). *Vision in Children*. Ontario, Canadian Deaf-Blind and Rubella Association.

Illingworth, W.M. (1910). *History of Education of the Blind*. London, Sampson Low.

Illuminating Engineering Society (1977). *Code for Interior Lighting*. London, IES.

Jamieson, M. *et al*. (1977). *Towards Integration*. Windsor, NFER.

Jan, J. *et al*. (1977). *Visual Impairment in Children and Adolescents*. London, Grune & Stratton.

Joint Committee of the College of Teachers of the Blind, and the National

Institute for the Blind (1936). *The Education of the Blind: A Survey*. London, E.J. Arnold.

Jose, R. (1983). *Understanding Low Vision*. New York, American Foundation for the Blind.

Klemtz, A. (1977). *Blindness and Partial Sight*. Cambridge, Woodhead-Faulkner.

Langley, B. (1981). *Functional Vision Inventory*. Chicago, Stoelting.

Lindstedt, E. and Hyvarinen, L. (1983). *BUST-LH Playful Vision Testing*. Stockholm, Elisgn.

Lomas, A.L. (1986). 'The Leeds peripatetic service for the visually handicapped'. University of Birmingham, B. Phil. (ed.) dissertation.

Longhorn, F. (1988). *Planning a Sensory Curriculum for the Very Special Child*. London, Souvenir Press.

Loomis, J.M. (1981). 'Tactile pattern perception', *Perception* 10: 5–27.

Lorimer, J. (1962). *Lorimer Braille Recognition Test*. Liverpool, College of Teachers of the Blind.

Lorimer, J. (1977). *A Short Course to Improve Braille Reading Efficiency*. Research Centre for Education of the Visually Handicapped, University of Birmingham.

Lowenfeld, B. (1950). 'Psychological foundations of special methods in teaching blind children'. In P.A. Zahl (ed.), *Blindness*. Princeton, Princeton University Press.

Lowenfeld, B. (1971). *Our Blind Children*. Springfield, Charles Thomas.

McInnes, J.M. and Treffry, J.A. (1982). *Deaf-blind Infants and Children*. Milton Keynes, Open University Press.

Mangold, S.S. and Olson, M.R. (1981). *Guidelines and Games for Teaching Efficient Braille Reading*. New York, American Foundation for the Blind.

Marshall, G.H. (1979). *The Eyes and Vision*. Coventry, Exhall Grange School.

Millar, S. (1985). 'Perception of complex patterns by touch', *Perception* 14: 293–303.

Millar, T. (1986). 'Factors involved in supporting visually impaired children in mainstream schools', *Support for Learning* 1(4): 16–21.

Mills, A. (ed.) (1983). *Language Acquisition in the Blind Child*. London, Croom Helm.

Murphy, F.M. and O'Driscoll, M. (1989). 'Observations on the motor development of visually impaired children', *Physiotherapy* 75(9): 505–8.

Nielsen, L. (1979). *The Comprehending Hand*. Copenhagen, National Board of Social Welfare.

Nielsen, L. (1988). *Multi-handicapped Children*. Realities and Opportunities; Proceedings of the International Symposium on Visually Handicapped Infants and Children, Edinburgh, ICEVH 1988.

Norris, M. *et al.* (1957). *Blindness in Children*. Chicago, University of Chicago Press.

Norris, N. (1972). *Aims and Methods in the Teaching of English to the Visually Handicapped*. Research Centre for Education of the Visually Handicapped, University of Birmingham.

Phillips, R.C. (1938). *A History of Royal Victoria School for the Blind 1838–1938* (unpublished).

Poland, D.J. and Doebler, L.K. (1980). 'Effects of black light visual field on eye contact training of spastic c.p. children', *Perceptual and Motor Skills* 51(1): 335–7.

Potenski, D.H. (1983). 'Use of black light in training retarded multiply handicapped, deaf-blind children', *Journal of Visual Impairment and Blindness* 77(10): 347–8.

Reynell, J. (1978). 'Developmental patterns of visually handicapped children', *Child: Care, Health and Development* 4: 291–303.

Reynell, J. and Zinkin, P. (1979). *Manual for the Reynell-Zinkin Scale*. Windsor, NFER.

RNIB (1985). *Initial Demographic Study*. Report by Shankland Cox Partnership. London, Royal National Institute for the Blind.

RNIB (1985). *Second Demographic Study: Visually-Handicapped Children*. England: Report by Shankland Cox Partnership. London, Royal National Institute for the Blind.

RNIB (1985). *Third Demographic Study: Visually-Handicapped People with Additional Disabilities*. England: Report by Jennifer Moss. London, Royal National Institute for the Blind.

Scholl, G.T. (1986). *Foundations of Education for Blind and Visually Handicapped Children and Youth: Theory and Practice*. New York, American Foundation for the Blind.

Smith, A.J. and Cote, K.S. (1982). *Look At Me*. Philadelphia, PA, Pennsylvania College of Optometry Press.

Sonksen, P.M. *et al.* (1984). 'Identification of constraints on motor development in young visually disabled children', *Child: Care, Health and Development* 70(10): 273–86.

Stocker, C.S. (1973). *Listening for the Visually Impaired*. Springfield, Ill., Charles Thomas.

Stone, J. (1988). 'Can't I finish the story? Teaching braille to infants', *British Journal of Visual Impairment* VI(2): 51–5.

Swann, W. (1981). *The Practice of Special Education*. Milton Keynes, Open University Press.

Taylor, H.S. (1986). *Guidelines for Primary Teachers*. Manchester, Shawgrove School.

Tobin, M.J. and Chapman, E.K. (1989). *Look and Think Handbook and Teacher's File*. London, Schools Council and Royal National Institute for the Blind.

Tooze, D. (1981). *Independence Training for Visually Handicapped Children*. London, Croom Helm.

Trowald, N. (1975). 'Learning strategies for blind listeners', *Report 66*. London, South Regional Association for the Blind, 115–27.

Urwin, C. (1988). 'The development and communication between blind infants and their parents'. In A. Lock (ed.), *Action, Gestures and Symbols*. San Diego, Calif., Academic Press.

Vernon, M.D. (1972). *Education of the Visually Handicapped*. London, DES.

Warburg, M. (1986). 'Medical and ophthalmological aspects of visual impairment in mentally handicapped people. In D. Ellis (ed.), *Sensory Impairments in Mentally Handicapped People*. London, Croom Helm.

Warburg, M. *et al.* (1979). 'Blindness among 7700 mentally retarded children in Denmark'. In V. Smith and J. Keen (eds), *Visual Handicap in Children*. London, Heinemann.

Warren, D.H. (1984). *Blindness and Early Childhood Development*. New York, American Foundation for the Blind.

Welsh, R.L. and Blasch, B.B. (1980). *Foundations of Orientation and Mobility*. New York, American Foundation for the Blind.

Wills, D. (1981). 'Notes on the application of the diagnostic profile to young blind children', *Psychoanalytic Study of the Child*. New Haven, Conn., Yale University Press.

Woods, D. (1979). 'The visually handicapped child'. In L. Groves (ed.), *Physical Education for Children with Special Needs*. Cambridge, Cambridge University Press.

Young, (1982). 'Asymmetry of cerebral hemispheric function during development'. In J.W.T. Dickerson and H. McGurk (eds), *Brain and Behaviour*. Glasgow, Blackie.

Index